The Castle of Dreams

The Castle of Dreams

Donna Fletcher Crow

Tyndale House Publishers, Inc.
Wheaton, Illinois

Cover illustration copyright © 1992 by Morgan Weistling

Scripture quotations are taken from the *New English Bible,* Copyright ©
1961, 1970, The Delegates of the Oxford University Press and the
Syndics of the Cambridge University Press; or from the *Holy Bible,* King
James Version.

Library of Congress Cataloging-in-Publication Data
Crow, Donna Fletcher.
    The castle of dreams / Donna Fletcher Crow.
        p.   cm. — (Intrigues ; 1)
    ISBN 0-8423-1068-1
    I. Title.   II. Series.
PS3553.R5872C3   1992
813'.54—dc20   92-5352

Printed in the United States of America
99   98   97   96   95   94   93   92
9   8   7   6   5   4   3   2   1

For fellow mystery fans,
Gaymon and Evelyn Bennett—
"Old friends are best"

Thank you to
Erwin Sonnenberg, Ada County Coroner;
Bob Mack, Detective, Boise Police Department;
Rick Groff, Manager, State Criminalistics Lab;
and *Bob Martin*, Forensic Toxicologist.

The Knowing

Between the dream and the reality,
from the coming of the light
to the falling of the dark,
from the openness of the truth
to the hiddenness of the lie,
there lurks the question.

Between the dream and the reality,
from the dawning of the day
to the closing of the night,
from the glory of the cross
to the depth of the pit,
there falls the shadow.

Between the dream and the reality,
from the clear-sightedness of waking
to the oblivion of sleeping,
from the doubt of the question
to the certainty of the knowing,
there cuts the truth.

And the truth shall make you free.

The Cast

At the Eyrie	In "Death By Candlelight"
Elizabeth Allerton	Sir Linden Leigh
Richard Spenser	Gloria Glitz
Sir Gavin Kendall	Nigel Cass
Irene North	Brian Rielly
Benton North	Suzanna Sweetly
Helen Johnson	Millie Maeda
Bill Johnson	Scott of the Yard
Cathy Johnson	
Evan Johnson	
Anita Crocker	
Weldon Stark	
Dr. Pearsall	
Mr. Hamlin	
Charles Parkerson	

Prologue

"No, Richard, I won't marry you." Elizabeth Allerton laughed and shook her head. "You are my best friend in the world. I thank the Lord for our friendship every day, and I want it to stay that way—friends. I don't want to get married."

"I didn't suppose you would, but it seemed worth a try." Richard Spenser absentmindedly moved a paper on his desk.

"I know, you hadn't asked me yet this week . . . "

"That's right, and here you were, asking a favor of me—I might never have you at so vulnerable a point again."

"Richard, I'm not asking a favor." Elizabeth brandished an exclusive mail-order catalog. "I'm urging this for your sake. Being the recognized authority on Sayers' Dante, drama, and theology still only makes you half a man. You need rounding out."

"And attending this mystery-week caper will do the rounding?" He pulled off his reading glasses and dropped them on top of the stack of papers he was grading.

"It's a start. It'll give you a feel for the whole whodunit thing."

He shook his head. "I knew you should never have added that course on mystery writing to the curriculum—even if I do have to admit you were a sellout."

She smiled, brushing back her short dark hair. "Nice to hear you admit it. But now, look. Concentrate on what I'm saying." She shoved the magazine under his nose. "Sir Gavin Kendall is going to be there. How can you possibly turn down an opportunity like this? Why, he's practically your opposite number—"

"Opposite number?" Richard looked at her dubiously.

"You really are hopeless." She threw up her hands. "Opposite number—like in a spy movie—the foreign agent whose work corresponds to yours."

Richard picked up a red pencil. "Your references are obtuse, Dr. Allerton. I don't read Sayers mysteries and I don't read Le Carré spy thrillers."

"That's precisely my point. Sir Gavin is the expert on Sayers' mysteries and that whole period. All of his books are written in Sayers' style, and he's writing a biography of Lord Peter Wimsey. Think of the opportunity—why, even if you went to England to interview Sir Gavin you'd only get a few hours of his time. Well, here he's going to be just eighty miles from us in the Rockies, and you could have a *whole week* to talk to him. Besides—," she gave her argument all she had, knowing Richard's patience for listening would soon wear thin—"the whole week is role-played as if it were 1933 on an English country estate. So you see, you wouldn't have to read the books. You could *experience* them . . . and it comes right at spring break time . . . and—"

Richard took the catalog from her hand and turned it over. "November? This thing's four months old—the reservations will have been gone long ago. Why are you pestering me with a Christmas item?"

"Well, I got a little behind in my catalog reading, but the timing is probably perfect. They've undoubtedly had cancellations by now, so we'll be able to get in."

"I always knew your passion for catalogs would come to no good." Richard replaced his glasses and picked up a paper. "In light of the fact that we're four months late, I think I'm safe enough to agree to try."

Knowing she'd won, Elizabeth slipped from the office, victory shining in her dark eyes. Of course, as head of the English department at Rocky Mountain Christian College, she could simply have ordered Dr. Spenser to do this. She wouldn't have done that, though. She far preferred to keep their relationship on the friendly basis that it had been ever since he came there from another part of the state three years ago. She enjoyed their friendship and their good-natured bantering.

She knew Richard understood their friendship and that his proposals were more out of

habit than anything else. That was why she
always laughed at them. Actually, she felt secretly
flattered when he proposed—he *was* a most eligi-
ble bachelor: intelligent, well established, stable,
a man of strong faith. All were factors that Elizabeth looked for in the man she would one day
marry. Still, she couldn't take Richard seriously
. . . and that worried her because she didn't want
to hurt him.

Sometimes she thought he actually meant his
proposals—he said he did. But no matter how
much she enjoyed working with him, no matter
how much she respected his scholarship and
Christian life or valued the pleasure they took in
many of the same things, she could never marry
a man who was so basically boring. Pity, too,
because he was awfully good-looking—in a
quiet, tweedy sort of way. What with his strong
cheek bones, thick brown hair, and gentle
humorous eyes, he had plenty of female students
vying for front row seats in his classes. . . .

She picked up the phone and punched out the
toll-free number for catalog orders.

1

Monday

Little rivulets of melted snow were rushing everywhere down the hillside, and here and there among the patches of tender spring grass, early snowdrops, wild crocus, and Grecian wind-flowers were blooming on the lower slopes of the mountain. As she and Richard drove through the tiny village of Hidden Glenn and headed north into the Rockies, Elizabeth suddenly felt the thrill of the adventure ahead of them—a whole week away from books and papers and students. A whole week at a beautiful mountain resort playing a sophisticated game in the style of her favorite reading! She clasped her hands and took a deep, happy breath. "Oh, thank you, God! Thank you," she said with a sigh.

Richard looked at her with a small smile. "I'll have to confess to some sense of anticipation about all this, too. You did take care of the costume bit, didn't you?"

"What do you think that enormous clothes bag was that you put in the trunk? The body for the mystery? I even paid the rental deposit out of my own pocket—but don't worry, I'll get you back later."

"I suppose it'll be all right. Of course, the brochure said daytime costumes were optional . . ." He hesitated.

"Optional, but fun. I'm even planning to change for afternoon tea."

He shook his head and guided the car around a sharp bend in the narrow, stone-edged road. "I never did know you to do anything by halves. What did you get for me, a deerstalker and an inverness cape?"

"Shows how much you know. Sherlock Holmes was *Victorian*. I got ascots to go with your tweed jacket and blazer for daytime and very, very formal wear for evening—real Fred Astaire."

"Yes, well—" Whatever comment he had been planning to make about her wardrobe plans was interrupted by their arrival at the gateway to Eyrie House. They were still at the base of the mountain, two and a half miles from the mansion-cum-hotel that was their destination, but they had to stop and be checked in here. "Registered Guests Only beyond This Point," the sign said. The guard found their names on the list and waved them on. "Have a nice week."

Although they were nearly above the timberline, a few pines grew on the sheltered side of the mountain and clumps of Colorado aspen were nearing bud. "In another month everything will be green." Elizabeth looked around her with satisfaction. "But right now I like the bare branches, a bit of starkness adds to the sense of mystery." Shadows from the bare trees fell across the narrow road like zebra stripes on a UPC code.

Another bend in the road and they were driving between massive granite outcroppings. "It's like driving through a rock quarry," Richard mused.

And then, past the rocks, Richard pointed almost straight up. "There it is."

The turrets, towers, and jutting angles of the stone castle sat on the top of the mountain like something straight out of a fantasy. "No wonder they named it Eyrie House," Elizabeth said. "Only an eagle could nest there." She shivered. "What a place for a mystery. *Brrrrr,* shades of 'Night on Bald Mountain.'"

And, as if on cue, a clap of thunder shook the ground.

"Mmm, that was close," Richard said. "Looks like we may be in for one of our famous, quick-gathering cloudbursts."

Elizabeth looked at the dark clouds gathering

in the evening sky, then back to the mountaintop fortress. "How did a castle get there?"

Richard smiled his slow smile. "I thought you were the expert on this venture."

"As I tell my students all the time—best way to learn things is to ask questions. Besides, you're the native Coloradan."

"True. Well, the original part was built before the turn of the century by a New York banker and railroad magnate who wanted to move west and needed an enticement to get his society wife to go with him."

"Did it work?"

"Oh, she moved with him all right, but she didn't stay long. Too, too boring. And the servant problem, my dear."

"What a shame, after he did all that for her. She must not have really loved him."

"Love would overcome any hardship—even boredom?" Richard cast her a sideways glance.

"Of course it would!" She spoke fervently, then blushed at the personal application of her comment. "Besides," she added hurriedly, "there couldn't have been many hardships living in a castle."

Once inside the castle, Elizabeth was even more convinced that life there could have been neither hard nor boring. Wide oak staircases zigzagged in every direction, leading hotel guests and staff to its multitude of corridors, all adorned with the original artwork and furniture of the castle. Victorian loveseats, velvet chairs, and little marble tables filled every nook and alcove. An abundance of fireplaces attested to the original method of heating the building, and out every window a breathtaking panorama reminded the visitors of their hilltop perch.

"Richard Spenser and Elizabeth Allerton." Richard gave their names to the desk clerk, who shuffled through a file of papers.

"Ah, yes, Dr. Spenser. A tower sitting room and adjoining bedroom with bath for Miss Allerton, a neighboring bedroom with bath for you. I must apologize, you will be in the north wing, which we had closed off for refurbishing. But we did wind up rather overbooked for this week, so the management decided to open a few rooms there rather than disappoint our late registrants. I hope you enjoy your stay with us."

Richard was just signing the register when a soft gong sounded from upstairs. "Half an hour until dinner," the desk clerk said.

Richard started to suggest they go straight up to the dining room, but Elizabeth had no intention of appearing at dinner the first night in a skirt and blouse she had been traveling in all afternoon. "You have no idea how quickly I can change," she said over her shoulder as she hurried off after the porter. They followed him up three flights of the zigzagging stairs, then down a long corridor with an uneven floor before

opening a door which led off into another hallway.

"You're the only ones in this wing so far," the
bellboy commented as he opened the door to
Elizabeth's room. "I hope you like it nice and
quiet."

"This will be fine," Richard said. Elizabeth
glanced down the hallway before entering her
room. Just beyond Richard's room was a parlor,
complete with a fireplace and cozy furniture. She
turned to inspect her own room—in need of
refurbishing, but the view, even through the rain
pelting the windows, was magnificent. The
antique furniture looked genuine, and there was
already a fire laid in the fireplace in the sitting
room.

"No television—hurrah! And I love the wind
whistling at the windows—makes it all seem
more mysterious." Elizabeth clapped her hands
together.

Richard tipped the porter, then picked up Elizabeth's large case and carried it into her room.
He glanced at his watch, then at her. "Fifteen
minutes," he said, heading for his room.

"I can do it in ten." She shut her door behind
him.

One reason she was so sure of herself was the
superb forethought and organization she had
put into her packing. She had approached this
with the same thoroughness she would have
applied to planning a semester syllabus: she'd

made a detailed list of the outfits she planned to wear for each activity listed in the advertisement, complete with accessories, including the hair ornaments that were so important to the fashionable woman of the thirties. Tonight's schedule called for the iced aqua crepe evening pajamas she had made from a long skirt that had been hanging in the back of her closet untouched for at least two years. She smiled as she pulled the deeply cowled top over her head. There were advantages to being a laggard about cleaning out one's closet. Instead of wearing the matching sash at her waist, she twisted it around her short dark hair in a demi-turban and fastened it with a large starburst of pearls and brilliants. A long rope of pearls was the perfect finishing touch. She glanced at her watch— three minutes left. She'd show Dr. Richard Spenser and his stopwatch brain.

Grabbing her toiletries case, she gave a sharp twist to her bathroom door, which didn't budge. "Oh, come on, don't stick on me!" She twisted and rattled the knob. "Well, now we know why you were scheduled to be redone." She restrained her impulse to give it a parting kick and went to Richard's room.

Richard was ready, but at least he wasn't looking at his watch. "Richard, I'll have to use your washroom; the door to mine's stuck."

She was so intent on beating his deadline, she hardly gave him a glance as she hurried across the gray carpet. But ninety seconds later, when she emerged with clean hands and powdered nose, she stopped, speechless, before the sight of Richard in a tuxedo. Her first thought was *He doesn't look boring in that.*

"I trust this is what I was supposed to wear tonight?" He adjusted his black bow tie.

"Yes, well done." She still stared at him. "I've never seen you in anything but tweeds and sweaters . . . absolutely stunning," she finished almost under her breath.

"I don't suppose you're stunned enough to accept my hand in marriage?" He said it lightly and her negative reply was equally light, but the fact that she knew he meant it made her pause. *Dear Lord, don't let me hurt him.*

Ever since Richard had joined the faculty at Rocky Mountain Christian College three years ago, shortly after his wife's death, everyone on the campus had hinted that the results would be inevitable. Certainly, Elizabeth admitted, she and Richard worked together perfectly . . . and there was no one she admired more . . . and he had so many of the qualities she would want in a husband . . . but the fact remained that he didn't do anything for her. She didn't require swooning in his presence, or losing her appetite, or waking in the middle of the night with his name on her lips, or any other such fictional nonsense. But there should be some quickening of the pulses when he came into the room, shouldn't there?

Some longing to have him put his arms around her, some vision of doing something with him besides discussing literature and curriculum.

Although tonight, she thought as she preceded him out the door, *he did make me catch my breath.*

They stopped at a table in one of the small sitting rooms near the dining parlor to receive their team assignments. These were the people with whom they would be working all week to solve the mystery. "You'll be with Blithe Spirit," the girl behind the table said as she handed them name badges with line drawings of the characters from the Noel Coward play. "All the teams are named for hit plays of the thirties," she went on. "The maître d' will show you to your table . . . you always eat with your group." They turned to go. "And good luck," the girl added.

Although the room had been expanded to several times its original size, Elizabeth had no trouble feeling she really was in a Jacobean dining room in an elegant country estate in England. As the waiter led them across the parquet floor, she admired the rich wood paneling on the walls, and the ornately molded plaster ceiling. There were just three empty seats at the large round table near the great, copper-hooded, stone fireplace.

"Oh, good; when we saw you come in we hoped you'd be in our group," a bright-eyed young woman greeted them. "We love your costumes."

Smiling, Richard and Elizabeth sat at the table and introduced themselves to their teammates. The buzz in the room indicated everyone at the other tables was doing the same. The friendly young lady who had greeted them introduced herself as Irene North, an aspiring actress who had many bit roles in well-known television programs to her credit. She then presented her gray-haired father, Benton, a Hollywood attorney. Next to him were Helen and Bill Johnson, from Phoenix, who had their teenage children Cathy and Evan with them. "What a fun thing to do for a family vacation!" The whole family beamed in agreement with Elizabeth's comment. Next to Richard was a stunning single woman whose sleek black hair reflected lights from the fireplace as she introduced herself as Anita Crocker.

"I wonder which celebrity we'll get?" Irene indicated four men and three women in vintage dress circulating among the tables in the roles of host and hostess.

"I've never been to one of these mystery weeks," Elizabeth said. "Does anyone know how it works?"

"See the tall man in the white dinner jacket?" Irene directed Elizabeth's gaze to a bald man with wire-rimmed glasses. He was talking to a team several tables to their right. "That's Weldon

Stark. He wrote the scenario and will be calling the shots all week."

Elizabeth turned in her chair. "Oh, so that's Weldon Stark. Have you read any of his books?"

"No, but I've seen the three that were made into movies," Irene said.

"I read *The Cold Corpse,*" Evan Johnson said. "It was awesome; lots of blood." His sister made a face at him, which undoubtedly was his aim.

"Have you come to one of these weeks before?" Elizabeth asked Irene.

"No, but I've read a lot about them. Tonight they act out the murder for us, then we have all week to interview the suspects and look for clues. When we think we have it solved, we work out a skit to present on Sunday morning. The winning team gets to come back next year."

"Yeah, and *we're* going to win!" Everyone at the table agreed enthusiastically with Evan's confident proclamation.

Elizabeth was suddenly aware of the gold-jacketed waiter standing by to take her order, so she picked up her menu, which was printed under the crest of their fictional residence, Kilcliffe Manor House. "I'll have the cold entree—avocado filled with lobster, shrimp, and crab . . . "

Elizabeth's voice trailed off as their host celebrity approached. After three attempts to get Elizabeth to state her preference of vegetables, the waiter moved down the table, leaving her in her state of oblivion. To Elizabeth's mind it was as if her favorite novels had fallen open at her feet and the characters of Albert Campion, Roderick Alleyn, and Lord Peter Wimsey had stepped full-blown from their pages all in one glorious person. Even if she hadn't been completely infatuated with the fictional heroes upon whom he was modeling his characterization, Elizabeth would have been captivated by Sir Gavin Kendall. His blond, aristocratic Anglo-Saxon looks; the perfectly tailored evening clothes on his tall frame; his easy, flawless manners as he greeted each one at their table . . . everything about the man seemed to be the total embodiment of all her dreams.

Elizabeth was last to receive his greetings. "I say, it's most frightfully nice to meet you." Holding his eyepiece in his left hand, he extended his right to Elizabeth. As his blue eyes met hers and his long fingers closed over her hand, her heart gave a lurch and she knew . . .

She hadn't been wrong to hold out for an experience more stirring than she'd had with Richard. All the things the poets had written through all the ages were true: Her heart thumped, her knees felt weak, her lungs forgot to breathe.

She had found the man she'd been waiting for.

2

After what seemed like an eternity, Elizabeth's heart left her throat so she could speak. "Thank you, Sir Gavin—or should we call you Lord Peter?"

"Oh, Gavin, please." He pulled out the empty chair next to Elizabeth's and folded himself into it. "The Wimsey/Poirot bit's just to get me into the role-playing thing. Actually, the chap I play is named Linden Leigh. It should be listed on your program."

Glad for something to do with her hands, Elizabeth turned to the back of the printed sheet while reminding herself to breathe. "Oh, yes, here's the whole cast. And one of you did it?"

"Ah, yes, murder most foul, to be enacted before your very eyes tonight."

While Sir Gavin discussed the roast beef with the waiter, Elizabeth studied the cast of suspects: Sir Linden Leigh, a British mystery writer; Gloria Glitz, a glamorous actress; Nigel Cass, a well-known theatrical agent; Brian Rielly, an international playboy; Suzanna Sweetly, a supporting actress; and Millie Maeda, companion and maid to Miss Glitz.

"Have any ideas?" Gavin returned his attention to Elizabeth.

She laughed. "How can I? I don't even know who the victim is yet. Do you know?"

"Oh, yes. The cast assembled yesterday for rehearsal and full instructions."

"Stark's famous for his intricate plots in his books. I suppose this will be that way, too."

Gavin raised one eyebrow. "The most comfort I can give you is my assurance that it's somewhat less complicated than the Talmud."

The throaty, masculine laughter on her right reminded Elizabeth that there were others at the table. "Oh, Sir Gavin, my colleague, Dr. Richard Spenser, is looking forward to talking with you this week . . . "

She turned the two men over to each other, happy to let them talk around her—Dante on her right, Wimsey on her left. It was a conversation she would normally have been thrilled to join, but now she needed the time to think. Unfortunately, thinking seemed to be the one thing she was incapable of doing. What was it people always said of Lord Peter? The essence of the English gentleman? Well, here he was—not in the pages of a book, but sitting beside her, in flesh and blood, eating roast beef and Yorkshire pudding.

"Excuse me, please. We're sorry to interrupt, but we wondered if we might take your pictures?" Two women from a nearby table stood before them clutching their cameras. "Your costumes are the best in the room."

The request seemed to include the three of them, so obligingly, Richard and Sir Gavin stood—with Elizabeth in the middle—and posed and smiled and said "Thank you" and "You're welcome" about six times.

The last bites of the velvety chocolate mousse cakes served at each table had barely had time to slide down the throats of the satisfied guests when Weldon Stark went to the microphone. He welcomed the company of international supersleuths assembled at Kilcliffe Manor House to solve the questions surrounding the death of one of England's most glamorous ladies. "While our cast is assembling to reenact the crime for you," he said, indicating the formally laid dinner table on a raised dais at the front of the room, "I want to give the proper credit due to my friend Sir Gavin Kendall for the crime's inception. Two years ago I was in London researching background for a book, and Sir Gavin took me to dinner at his club. Over some excellent brandy we began trading mystery plot ideas. I will admit that each plot seemed to improve with each brandy. . ." The audience laughed, and Stark continued, "What you are about to witness tonight, ladies and gentlemen, is 'Death by Candlelight,' as conceived by Sir Gavin Kendall and a bottle and a half of brandy, and adapted by Weldon Stark."

The audience applauded as a spotlight was turned on the table. Elizabeth reached for her notepad and pen, as others were doing. It would be essential to catch all the details of what they were about to see in order to solve the mystery.

Weldon Stark narrated: "It is March 15, 1933, and the Ides of March are upon the elegant, but faded, Yorkshire estate of theatrical agent Nigel Cass. It is there that he is hosting a weekend party to celebrate the engagement of the glamorous actress Gloria Glitz to peer of the realm and best-selling mystery writer Sir Linden Leigh."

Nigel entered the stage, escorting a stunning blond. She wore a clinging gold dress, which revealed a back bared to below the waistline when she turned to greet her fiancé with a kiss.

"A violent spring storm has swept across the moor, cutting off electricity and phone service, and isolating the mansion and its inhabitants." The thunder produced by the technicians was made even more realistic by the actual rain cascading down the windows of the dining room.

At the entrance of a maid wearing a black dress and white ruffled apron and cap, Stark continued, "Millie Maeda, Gloria's maid and companion, will have to wait on the table tonight because the other servants were stranded in town when the storm broke unexpectedly."

Millie announced the entrance of the remaining guests: "Miss Suzanna Sweetly and Mister Brian Rielly." The platinum Suzanna in a pale blue chiffon gown was moonlight eclipsed by the golden sun that was Gloria Glitz. Susie's companion, in a ruffled evening shirt and continental hairstyle, kissed the ladies' hands and bowed to the men before the guests moved to the table. Nigel, as host, sat at the head with Gloria, the guest of honor, on his right, and Suzanna to his left. Sir Linden sat next to Gloria; Brian next to Suzanna.

As soon as the guests were seated, Nigel stood, holding the glass of champagne Millie had just served, and offered the toast. "My friends, we are here to celebrate the happy event of the engagement of Miss Gloria Glitz and Sir Linden Leigh, two of the brightest lights of the London social world. Long may they shine together." Sir Linden smiled at his betrothed and absentmindedly ran his finger around the rim of his wine glass during the speech. "To the happy pair!" Nigel finished.

With cries of "Hear, hear!" and "The happy pair!" Susie and Brian drank while Gloria and Linden rose to acknowledge the toast.

"And to our friends." Sir Linden raised his glass.

"Our friends," Gloria agreed. They each put their glasses to their lips then, linking arms, took a sip from each other's glass.

In a rush of excitement, Suzanna jumped from her chair and ran to embrace Gloria. "I'm so happy for you, darling!" And for just an instant Susie's hand paused above Gloria's water goblet.

The company returned to their seats, and Millie served the Almond Cream soup that had been waiting in a tureen on the sideboard. Brian was the last to be served. Just as Millie reached over his shoulder with the round, flat soup plate, he turned and bumped her, sending the thick creamy liquid down the front of his ruffled shirt. Susie gave a cry of dismay and Millie said over and over, her cockney accent thick, "I'm ever so sorry, sir. Reelly I am, ever so sorry."

In the scramble of solicitude over Brian's shirt, Brian exchanged napkins with Gloria. To add to the general confusion, Linden, in handing his napkin across to Brian, tipped over his champagne glass. "Millie, clear this away and bring me a fresh drink!" Linden barked. Millie, glad for an excuse to be removed from the soup-spilling scene, was quick to obey.

With order finally restored, Gloria turned to Nigel. "Well, darling, do you think it would be safe to ask you to pass the relishes?"

"I shall attempt to do so without mishap. If you will allow me . . . " With a flourish he selected the largest stalk of celery, sprinkled salt on it, and presented it to Gloria. "You see, my dear, I haven't been your agent for all these years without learning how you fancy your celery."

For a moment all was quiet while the guests ate. Gloria took a spoonful of soup, then a bite of celery, wiped her mouth on the napkin, and sipped from her water goblet. At a sign from Nigel, Millie removed the soup plates and began serving the lobster medallions en gelée.

Suddenly Gloria broke the silence with a strangled choking sound. Her hands at her throat, she tried to cough. Her face turned a pale gray-blue (testimony to the expertise of the lighting technicians). Linden Leigh sprang to his feet. With his arms around Gloria's chest, he attempted to dislodge whatever was choking her. But, with aid once again from the lighting technicians, Gloria turned red and slumped forward.

Leigh continued his first-aid attempt, but at last Nigel picked up the limp, diamond-encircled wrist and after several seconds said, "I'm afraid it's no use, old boy."

Millie screamed. Susie fainted. The lights went out.

Weldon Stark's voice cut through the dark. "What killed Gloria Glitz?"

When the lights came on again the first to speak at the Blithe Spirit table was Irene. "Well, what do you think?"

Everyone leaned toward the center of the table, not wanting their comments to be overheard by a competing team.

"It looked like an accidental choking," Anita ventured.

"It also looked like everyone had an opportunity to poison her." Cathy Johnson voiced what Elizabeth's notes revealed.

"What about motive?"

"I can't wait to start interviewing suspects tomorrow—there was a lot more going on than met the eye, you can bet on that."

"I hope it wasn't in the soup—that's what I ordered for dinner."

"What do you think, Dr. Spenser?" Anita Crocker touched his arm.

"Call me Richard, please. Did you notice . . . ?" Elizabeth could hear no more as he turned to the woman beside him.

"Well played, Sir Linden," Bill Johnson greeted the return of their celebrity.

"Thanks, awfully. Good show, what?" He remained in character as he took his seat and accepted a cup of coffee from the waiter.

Elizabeth laughed. "You are a man of many parts, Sir Gavin Kendall, Albert Campion, Sir Linden Leigh . . . "

"Shhh," he silenced her, looking over his shoulder. "I say, one can't be too careful. Scotland Yard could be anywhere, and those fellows do get the wind up a bit about people running around under false identities. There's no end to the things they can—"

Gavin's banter was interrupted by a growling rumble that grew steadily louder like the approach of a freight train. The table shimmied. The whole room vibrated violently. Elizabeth felt Richard grab her shoulders and push her to the floor. "Get under the table," he ordered everyone around him.

It could have been no more than a minute or two that they crouched under the protection of the heavy oak table while the earth shook around them. But to Elizabeth, who was sure that at any moment the entire hotel would tumble from its perch, it seemed like hours.

With her eyes closed so tightly it almost stopped her breathing, she was thankful for the comfort of the masculine arm around her shoulders. But she was even more thankful for the answer that came to her terrified prayer for help: "He that dwelleth in the secret place of the most High shall abide under the shadow of the Almighty. . . ." The comforting words of Psalm 91 calmed her in spite of the continued trembling of the mountain. "He shall deliver thee from . . . the noisome pestilence. . . ." The roaring seemed to be receding, as if the freight train that hit them was rushing on down the tracks. "Thou shalt not be afraid for the terror by night."

The rumble had almost died away and the

quaking stilled when the lights went out, leaving the room in a blackness relieved only by the light of the fireplace and the flickering candles in the center of each table. Richard helped Elizabeth to her feet and righted her chair, which had been knocked over in the confusion. For a moment everyone was quiet, dazed by the experience. Then each person gave way to individual reactions: swearing, laughing, crying, talking. Elizabeth, who was trembling violently, suddenly became aware of the fact that she was gripping Richard's arm with both hands. "Oh, was I hurting you?"

"No, no. Of course not. Are you all right?"

Her trembling gave way to laughter, on the edge of hysteria. "I'm fine. Would you look at that—it didn't spill a drop of water." She pointed to the goblets on the table. "I didn't know Colorado had earthquakes. I've never been in one before."

"I have. Twice when I was in college in California. But it didn't feel like that." Richard helped Elizabeth to her chair. "I'm not sure it was an earthquake."

"Then what . . . ?"

A spoon banging on a glass at the front of the room turned everyone's attention to Weldon Stark who now had to speak to them without the aid of a microphone. "Well, how about that? Didn't we tell you we would spare no effort to bring you an exciting week?" The laughter was nervous, but it helped ease the tension.

"The management assures me that the hotel has its own emergency auxiliary power unit. Just as soon as they can get the coal-fired plant stoked up, we'll be in business again. In the meantime, we ask you to remain in your seats so no one will walk into any doors or anything. The house physician is here." A dim form next to Stark raised his hand. "If any of you received cuts or bruises, our charming young Dr. Pearsall will be glad to attend to you just as soon as the lights are on. And, ladies, he isn't married."

The lighthearted chatter helped soothe ragged nerves, and Stark had barely finished speaking when the chandeliers flickered on. Everyone's sigh of relief changed to disappointment, though, when they went out again. A minute later, the lights came on again and stayed on two or three seconds before going off. The third time, everyone held their breath, then gradually relaxed as the lights continued to glow steadily.

"Looks as though we're going to have light. Thank goodness for that, anyway." Richard turned to Gavin. "Would you like to come back to the room now and see that bibliography?" Gavin assented and they turned toward the corridor.

"Richard! You aren't going to work tonight,

are you?" Even as well as she knew what a one-track mind he had, this surprised her. He really was too much.

"This isn't work, it's fun. Besides, there may not be time later in the week."

She threw up her hands in surrender. "Gloria Glitz is murdered before our eyes, the whole hotel is practically thrown off the mountain in an earthquake or something, and you want to read a bibliography of thirteenth-century Latin sources."

"Certainly; it's at times like this one needs the still calm of the classics."

Elizabeth knew he was teasing her, so she quit arguing and walked along with the two men. After all, she had gotten Richard to come this week with arguments that it would be good for his work. "The reason I prefer the Sayers translation is that, in her hands, the universality of Dante's spiritual quest really comes alive. It's more than a translation; she shares his journey . . . "

Elizabeth smiled at Richard's words—she'd been right—he did need to balance his superb scholarship with a feel for more popular literature. She had heard Richard's speech before, so she let her mind wander back to the experience they had just been through. What a miracle that no one was seriously hurt! She hoped the old hotel hadn't received any structural damage. Although she was outwardly calm, she was filled with nervous excitement—the adrenaline level in her blood was probably high enough to make it unsafe for her to drive.

Slackening her pace, Elizabeth fell slightly behind her escorts so she could look at them. Both were tall and slim in classic formal wear; their heads, one dark and the other blond, were bent slightly together as they carried on their discussion. From outward appearance, there was no reason to prefer one infinitely over the other. Elizabeth frowned slightly. Why should Gavin make her breath race and her heart do flip-flops, while Richard did absolutely nothing to her? She remembered the arm that held her through the ordeal under the table—whose arm had it been? Richard had pushed her down to safety and helped her out, as he had the others nearby, but it seemed more likely that Gavin, the complete gentlemen, would be the one who would quietly support her.

"Where are you going?" Gavin's sharp inquiry cut through her thoughts.

She saw he was still in the main corridor, while Richard had turned into their wing. "That part of the hotel's closed off."

"Was," Richard replied. "They reopened it to accommodate the overflow crowd."

"Where is your room?" Elizabeth asked.

"Just down the hall and around the corner." Gavin pointed to the far end of the corridor. "But it's terrible, your having to stay here. Isn't it awfully uncomfortable? Drafty and that sort of thing?"

Elizabeth replied as Richard opened the door, "Not at all—except my bathroom door is stuck. Oh, I forgot to tell the desk clerk."

"Well, maybe this evening's excitement jarred it loose," Richard suggested as he turned to his briefcase to find the file he'd promised Gavin.

"Good idea, I'll check." Elizabeth smiled as she felt Sir Gavin's eyes on her while she left the room. "Oh, good, it has," she called to them. "The door's ajar."

She stepped into the white-tiled room, then froze. She felt all the blood drain from her head and a chill enter her entire body. She wanted to scream, but felt too faint. Clutching the wall, she backed into the sitting room. The men looked at her, startled.

"There's a man in my bathroom . . . ," she whispered. "I think he's . . . he's . . . "

And then everything went dark.

3

Tuesday

When Elizabeth came to, the house doctor was taking her pulse, and Gavin was standing at the end of the sofa, looking as stricken as she felt.

"My dear, I'm so sorry! We all are." Gavin knelt beside her, pushing the doctor out of the way. "I'm sure if Stark had had any idea it would be so upsetting he'd never have—"

"Stark? You mean that was part of the game?" Elizabeth sat up slowly, still feeling none too steady.

Richard came over to her. "Don't worry, I went straight for the doctor, and Kendall here made the guy clear out fast so you wouldn't be upset again."

"I certainly did. I sent him packing sharply and told him to tell Stark we shall have to omit that part from his script. We shall simply pretend it never happened."

27

"Oh, no, don't change the plan on my account. It was just the way it came after the earthquake and everything. I'm sure if I'd taken a second look I'd have realized . . . as it was, I thought—"

"What did you think?" Gavin asked.

"I'm not sure. I guess I thought he wandered in by mistake, and then the quake frightened him so much he had a heart attack . . . or he fell over and hit his head, or . . . I don't know. It sounds awfully silly now."

"Well, don't worry about it a bit. This is the last you'll hear of it, I assure you." Gavin gave her arm a gentle squeeze, then moved back to make room for Dr. Pearsall.

"I think you'll be fine now, Miss Allerton. But I'll leave these tablets with you in case you have trouble sleeping. If you have a headache or any problems in the morning, be sure to give me a call. It's after midnight now, so try to get some sleep."

Elizabeth didn't approve of taking sleeping pills, but by 4 A.M., after three hours of reliving walking into that room and finding a body in the bathtub . . . what a good actor that man was—so still and lying at such an odd angle . . . with a sigh she got up and swallowed the tablets. She wakened to a sun-streaked morning that made it hard to believe in the darkness and alarms of the night before. Elizabeth still felt a bit groggy after her drug-induced sleep, but the

bright color and flowing lines of her buttercup
and navy, dolman-sleeved tunic lifted her spirits.
She reached for the phone and dialed Richard's
room. "Wear your dark blue blazer, white
slacks, and yellow ascot," she told him.

"Yes, Mother," he replied. "As a matter of
fact, I did exactly that."

"Mmm, yes. You certainly did." She smiled
approvingly when she joined him a few minutes
later. "Can't have anyone saying your colleague
dresses you funny."

As soon as they started down the wide stair-
case they were greeted with the friendly sound
of the breakfast gong, and a little further along
with tantalizing aromas.

"Who was it that said England's major contri-
butions to civilization were the Magna Carta,
Shakespeare, and the English breakfast?" Richard asked.

Elizabeth breathed deeply and laughed.
"George Will, maybe? But I think he got them
in the wrong order."

No one would have argued with her when
they were served platters of grilled tomatoes
and mushrooms with toast, eggs, and plump,
juicy sausages that were sweet and spicy at the
same time.

"I can't wait to start interviewing witnesses,"
Irene said as she leaned across the table, her
eyes sparkling. "I have several theories already."

Elizabeth could see why Irene was an actress.

She wasn't really beautiful—she was short and slightly plump—but she had what they called "star quality." You just automatically looked at her when she talked. And her quiet father was so obviously proud of her. "What a special thing— for a father and daughter to take a vacation together. Wasn't your mother able to come?"

"No, my sister just had a baby, and Mom would much rather stay with the grandchildren. Daddy and I are the crime buffs in the family." Benton turned to smile at his daughter, and Elizabeth saw he was wearing a hearing aid. That was probably one reason he was so quiet.

Conversation at the tables stopped when Weldon Stark stood before the microphone. "Well, we now have an official report on that bit of unscheduled excitement last night. It seems that the rain yesterday washed out a large patch of loose rock and mud on the hillside.

"We've had quite a landslide down the road apiece. It took the phone and electricity wires with it, but we got a radio newscast from Hidden Glenn. Officials are aware of our predicament and will set to work digging us out as soon as possible. There was, however, considerable flooding in the valley, and those problems will have to be attended to first, since their situation is much more serious than ours." Stark waited for the buzz of conversation to die down before he continued.

"The hotel has assured me that we have plenty

of coal to keep the electricity humming for the rest of the week, if necessary. The kitchen is well stocked, and we see no reason everything shouldn't proceed just as scheduled. We are fortunate, I must say, that our staff was cut off on this side of the road, rather than in town as the Kilcliffe servants were. Millie would have her hands full trying to serve us all." The role-players laughed, and several applauded their waiters, who were refilling coffee cups.

"This morning the suspects will be available for interviewing. The ground rules are that all witnesses are to tell the truth except in matters relating directly to the murder. Except the murderer—that person may lie about anything."

The group at the table looked at each other with anticipation. "I want to know if Millie liked her mistress," Cathy Johnson said between bites of grilled tomato.

"Do you think Gloria and Brian were lovers?" Anita Crocker asked, and Elizabeth noted that it seemed she always directed her questions to Richard.

"I bet that other actress was jealous," Helen Johnson said, spreading lime marmalade on her toast.

"Probably, but what about the agent?"

"No, he had an incentive to keep her alive— she was his meal ticket," Irene said. "I know what my agent gets just for my bit stuff."

"Maybe she was going to fire him."

"Hold on a minute!" Benton held up a hand. "Sherlock Holmes says it's a capital mistake to theorize before having the facts."

"Sound advice. Let's go get organized." Richard put his coffee cup down and scooted back his chair, making a scraping noise on the wooden floor. "Shall we use the library for our meeting room?" The others assented, and he led the way.

Richard taped a hand-lettered sign to the door, labeling the library as the official meeting room for Blithe Spirit. "Now, who wants to interview whom this morning?"

Elizabeth wanted to interview Gavin, or rather Linden, who had breakfasted with the actors. But she didn't want to seem too eager, so she waited for the others to choose.

"Did you want to take Millie, Cathy?" Richard asked.

"Sure, Evan and I'll do her."

Helen and Bill offered to interview Suzanna.

"We'll tackle the agent. OK, Dad?" Irene said.

"Richard, would you help me question Brian? I'm sure we'll need a man's opinion, too." In fairness, Elizabeth had to admit that Anita didn't exactly bat her eyes at Richard, but the effect was the same.

Richard looked at his list. "Elizabeth, that leaves you to do Sir Linden. Do you mind?"

Mind? She gulped.

"No, that's fine. If he isn't too grief-stricken over the death of his fiancée, of course."

"That takes care of it, then. We'll meet back here after lunch with our reports." Elizabeth watched Richard leave the room with Anita. She was so tiny her head barely reached his shoulder, which gave her the advantage of always having to look way, way up at him when they talked. And he looked down and smiled.

Elizabeth couldn't wait to see Gavin this morning. She had glimpsed him across the breakfast room—in his light beige double-breasted suit and his blond hair brushed to an aristocratic sleekness, he looked more heroic than ever.

In the Fern Parlor, he was sitting in a wicker armchair by the fireplace, already answering a question put to him by a member of the Private Lives team. "Yes, yes, quite. It really was the most beastly experience. She was such a lovely girl, you know. Absolutely charming, and such talent . . . a terrible thing to have happen." He dropped his head in his hand, his long fingers running into his hair.

"Sir Linden, we do apologize for breaking in on your bereavement," another questioner began, "but would you tell us how long you and Miss Glitz had been dating?"

With a visible effort, the witness pulled himself together. "Gloria and I had been friends for years. We were in the same circle, you understand. But we had only been dating what you'd call seriously for nine or ten months."

How well he does this, Elizabeth thought. *It's impossible to believe he's acting.* She even felt a small stab of jealousy for the mourned Gloria.

"And did you have serious girlfriends before?" someone in the far corner asked.

"Oh, quite. But then, that depends on what you call serious, doesn't it?"

"Will you tell us about the one before Gloria Glitz?"

Sir Linden rubbed his chin thoughtfully. "I say, it's a little hard to remember. Well, now, yes, that would have been Lady Leila Landsbury, an old, old friend of the family—not that the lady herself was ancient, you understand."

Elizabeth introduced a new line of questioning, "Sir Linden, is your title inherited?"

"No, His Most Gracious Majesty King George V conferred this honor upon me in recognition of my contribution to English arts and letters."

"And how long have you held the title?"

"A little less than a year. Since the publication of *Clouds of Carcasses.*"

A woman next to Elizabeth took up the questioning, "That was your wildly successful best-seller?"

"Madam, how am I to maintain my decorum of British understatement if you will thrust such bouquets at me? But yes, His Majesty was good enough to mention that book in his charter of knighthood. I believe revenue from the foreign

publications of the book did make a certain contribution to the exchequer."

Elizabeth smiled as she scribbled notes. It
was fun to ponder the parallels between the real
man and the character he was portraying. Stark
must know him well. She didn't know much
about Sir Gavin Kendall beyond having read his
books, but she did know that his own best-
seller, *Who Doth Murder Sleep?* had actually
resulted in his knighthood. She didn't know
what he had written since, however. When she
had a chance, she would ask Sir Gavin what he
was working on now besides his fictional
Wimsey biography.

A woman wearing a Conversation Piece name
tag asked, "What were the autopsy results?"

"There was no autopsy, madam. The certificate of death listed natural causes, choking.
That's why I really don't see what all the fuss is
about."

"Was there anything at all unusual noted on
the certificate?"

"I don't really know what might be unusual.
I fortunately haven't had much experience in all
this, you understand."

"Yes, of course. But was there any more information at all?"

Leigh twirled his eyeglass on the end of its
ribbon. "I seem to remember some mention of
the deceased's complexion appearing cherry

red. I assume that's natural in choking cases. The constable made no suggestion of foul play."

"Was this constable an officer experienced in investigating sudden deaths?" The tweed-suited questioner moved closer to Sir Linden, who appeared rather bored by this line of questioning.

"He seemed a right enough old codger for a country constable. About ready for retirement, I'd guess. He'd probably seen his share of sudden deaths, natural and unnatural, in his time."

The questioning continued: No, he didn't have any theory about the murder. No, he didn't think Gloria was carrying on behind his back. No, he didn't murder her himself. The interview ended, they all moved toward the dining parlor for luncheon.

Surveying the salad bar, which ran the width of the room, Elizabeth remarked to Helen Johnson, "It appears Stark had it right when he said the kitchen was well supplied. I'm glad they had plenty of fresh things on hand."

Helen agreed, "I'd really forgotten all about the landslide. I suppose it doesn't make any difference, anyway. No one would want to go anywhere. Unless there was an emergency, of course."

"I think it just makes it all more realistic and exciting," Cathy said as she joined her mother. "Maybe we aren't cut off at all—maybe they just said that to make it feel more like the script."

Elizabeth laughed as she topped her salad with

cherry tomatoes. "That's an original idea, Cathy. You never know around here. That's why they call it a mystery week. As a matter of fact, last night I had a—"

"Hullo there, may I carry your plate to the table for you?"

"Oh, Sir Linden, how very democratic of you." She surrendered her plate. "Or are you Sir Gavin now? It's rather confusing."

"I'm me now, Gavin, to you." He set her plate on the table and pulled out her chair for her. "No aftershocks from last night, I hope?"

"None, thank you. I slept very well—thanks to the doctor's pills, I'll have to admit. Aren't you sitting down?"

"No, no. Some of the members might want to cast aspersions at Sir Linden, and we wouldn't want to inhibit them. I'll see you at tea in the Lake Lounge, right-o?"

"Fine. I'll look forward to it." She watched his broad-shouldered, well-tailored back retire to the far side of the room. "Did you and Evan have an interesting interview with the maid?" She turned to the teenagers beside her, leaving Anita and Richard with their heads together across the table.

"Ooh, yes. Let's eat fast—I can't wait to hear what everybody learned."

It seemed that the entire team shared Cathy's sentiment because in record time Blithe Spirit was assembled in the library, notebooks in front of them. Everyone looked to Richard, since, by common consent, he had become their leader. "Cathy, I think we'd better let you report before you burst. Do you think Millie put poison in the soup?"

"If she did, she got mixed up and served it to the wrong person. She was devoted to Gloria, but she hated Sir Linden—"

"She'd served Gloria ever since her first hit show years ago," Evan interrupted his sister. "She didn't think Leigh was nearly good enough for her mistress. She said," Evan consulted his notes to get the exact wording, "'Me mistress were a lovely loidy, and very talented. That there Sir Linden, as 'e called 'isself, 'ad as much talent as my Uncle Icabod. Not that I fancy myself much of a reader, you understand, but my sister Vicky as was 'is Lordship's secretary afore she died—'"

"Wait a minute!" Irene sat forward on the edge of her chair. "Gloria's maid's sister was Sir Linden's secretary?"

Cathy nodded. "Yes, but she died a couple of years ago."

"Aha!" Irene waved her pencil in the air. "Foul play—the plot thickens. Let's see, how could that tie in?"

"I don't think it does," Evan said. "Millie said her sister died of cancer."

But Irene was not to be deterred. "Yes, but

she could lie—if it related directly to the murder."

"Let's hear the rest of the reports before we try to formulate a theory," Richard said, cutting through all the supposings.

Anita flashed her brilliant smile. "Well, Richard and I learned some very interesting things about Brian. I think he's one of our prime suspects. He isn't just the playboy he pretends to be—he's really a British Secret Service agent. And he was Gloria's boyfriend before Linden. He admitted that they were very close. Now maybe—"

"So why would that make him a suspect if her loved her?" Benton North spoke up for the first time in the meeting. "Sounds like another motive for murdering Leigh. You don't suppose they got the wrong victim?"

"If so, then Linden Leigh is still in danger," Elizabeth said, "because the murderer is still with us."

"That's right, and we're with him—or her—all trapped here together, like in *Ten Little Indians* or something." Irene gave a dramatic shudder.

"Maybe that's it!" Cathy cried. "Wasn't one of those murders in that movie committed to cover up the real murderer and confuse everybody? Maybe our murderer killed Gloria as a distraction, and maybe he'll get the real target later."

"We've got to work fast," Evan said.

"Just a minute now, don't get carried away. We don't even know for sure that it was murder. Remember, Stark asked *what* killed Gloria Glitz, not *who.*" Richard, always the levelheaded one, calmed them. "Now, who interviewed Susie?"

"Bill and I did," Helen said. "Of course it was murder. Who ever read a mystery without a villain? And it seems like Susie had plenty of motive. She was repeatedly cast as Gloria's understudy and played supporting roles to Gloria's stardom. Susie got good reviews by the critics, but never could land a starring role ahead of Gloria."

"Yeah." Irene pulled a face. "I know the feeling."

Everyone laughed, and Bill continued their report. "That's not her only area of jealousy; she also thinks Sir Linden is wonderful and much too good for Gloria." He was interrupted with several *ah-ha*s. "But she denied wanting him for herself. She says she's in love with Brian."

"Yeah, but she could be lying."

"Did Brian say if he loved her?"

"We didn't ask."

"Was Nigel Susie's agent, too?"

Irene glanced at her notes. "No, I don't think so. Gloria was his only major client. He had handled her for ten years—ever since she was a struggling unknown. He devoted his career to her throughout her rise to stardom. He admitted he has done very well financially."

"Hmmm, what did he think about his star attraction getting married? Do we have another motive against Leigh?"

"No, he said he thought becoming Lady Leigh would be very good for her billing. Apparently she did, too. She didn't seem to have any intention of giving up her career."

"Were his accounts ever audited?"

"What were the terms of his contract with Gloria?"

"I wonder if he handled writers, too?"

"Yeah, did he ever represent Sir Linden?"

"OK," Richard called the group back to order. "Do we all have a list of the information we want to get at the next interviews? Do you want to take the same people again?"

The team decided it would be more beneficial to tackle different suspects, so assignments were made, and Elizabeth chose Millie. This time Richard volunteered to go with her.

" . . . that's right, Vicky always said she could write a better mystery than 'is sirship. 'So why don't you?' I asker, 'That'd settle 'is dust.' 'I just might at that,' she says . . . but then she died." Millie shook her head. "Powerful quick, she went, 'ardly no warnin' at all."

"What did Vicky think of *Clouds of Carcasses*? Didn't she think that was a good book?"

Millie continued to shake her head. "She was in 'er grave by then." As an afterthought she added, "But I 'aven't noticed 'im writing anything else people said were as good as that—even if all 'is books do sell a lot, 'is being such a big name and all."

"And you were unhappy about your mistress marrying Sir Linden?" Elizabeth prodded.

Millie sniffed. "'Is Lordship should 'ave married that Lady 'oity-toit 'e was going around with afore 'e sweet-talked me mistress into marryin' 'im. 'E never loved 'er, I'll warrant."

"Was Gloria generally popular? I mean, do you think most people were as genuinely fond of her as you were?" Richard asked.

"Them as wasn't jealous of 'er, like that there Suzanna Sweetly was. And then there was Mr. Cass—"

"Yes, what about Nigel Cass?" The questioners perked up their ears for a clue.

"I don't know much, but I know what I 'eard."

"And what was that?"

"Just that evening afore she died, 'er and Mr. Cass 'ad a fearful row in the library."

"Did you hear what was said?"

"Did she threaten to break her contract?"

Millie looked offended. "I 'ad me 'ands full serving the whole dinner with not so much as a kitchen skivvy to 'elp. I didn't 'ave no time to be listenin' at doors, now did I?"

"Hmmm, that's something to follow up on." Elizabeth marked the line in her notebook with a star.

Back in the library, Elizabeth found it difficult to keep her mind on everyone's report as she thought of her date with Gavin. But Irene had some exceedingly interesting new facts about Brian that caught her attention: "He admitted to committing certain indiscretions when he dated Gloria. I got the idea he tried to dazzle her with tales of his exploits and international connections, and probably told too much. Didn't you think so, Daddy?" She turned to her father.

"Yes, that's right. I asked him if he intentionally exchanged napkins with her at the dinner. He said he did."

Irene picked up her father's cue. "Yes, he said there was a message in it asking her to meet him in the conservatory after dinner so he could gain her assurance that his secrets were safe with her."

"Hmm, sounds like he was going to blackmail her or something—or she him. Now, how would that work?" Elizabeth wondered.

"Maybe that's just an excuse—an alibi—making it look like he wouldn't have killed her because he was planning to meet her after dinner," Irene said.

"Maybe she gave him some kind of signal

that she wouldn't meet him, so he killed her," Cathy suggested.

"How?"

"Er, well, I'll work it out."

"I still think there was poison on his napkin. Spies would have that sort of thing," Evan said with confidence.

"Well, Gavin said—," Anita stopped and laughed, "Oh, I mean *Linden* said he couldn't imagine how Millie got the ridiculous idea about her sister's opinion of his writing. As a matter of fact, Vicky had attempted to write a mystery herself and had repeatedly asked his advice. But nothing came of it."

"Because she died?"

"He said the book wouldn't have made it anyway. He said everyone thinks they can write just because they can speak the language—an idea as ridiculous as thinking they can dance with the Royal Ballet just because they can walk."

Several people started developing theories, but Elizabeth slipped out. She wanted to freshen up before tea. She had to laugh at herself for her hesitation before opening the bathroom door. She didn't want to find any more bodies in there—even one only impersonating a corpse.

4

Elizabeth slipped a headband around her
forehead so its yellow bangles hung just above
her left ear, then she took a quick glance in the
mirror on the back of her closet door. The lines
of her tunic top flowed to below her knees
above wide-legged trousers. *Thirties' styles are so
much fun,* she thought, then grabbed her tiny
clutch bag and skipped down the four flights of
stairs to the Lake Lounge where Gavin was waiting to take afternoon tea with her.

"I say, Tuppence, absolutely smashing," he
said. Elizabeth smiled delightedly as he bowed
over her hand, and they both laughed. It was
wonderful the way he knew all the stories she
loved, and the way he shared them with her
with such creative flair. For just a moment, she
felt as though she really was Tuppence, Agatha
Christie's heroine, and Sir Gavin was Tommy,
Tuppence's love.

Sir Gavin smiled at her, pulling her hand through his arm. "Thank goodness, we don't have to keep up this role business all the time. Just enough to keep the tourists happy, what?" He led her to a small, overstuffed sofa by the window. "All comfy, are you? I go to mount an attack on the tea trolley. I shall be bloody, bold, and resolute."

Elizabeth's laughter followed him all the way across the room. It was all such delicious nonsense. But the idea of playing Tuppence to his Tommy, or Harriet Vane to his Lord Peter, held far more than acting appeal for her. She had met him only the day before, and yet already felt she had always known him. In a way she had, in her dreams. The tall, polished aristocrat. Intellectual and yet fun, immaculately dressed and yet relaxed, warm and friendly to everybody and at the same time focused on her.

She had always believed firmly in God's guidance and in the perfection of his timing, that he would open the right doors for her at the right time. That was one reason she was able to give herself so totally to her teaching position that she had been promoted to department head at the startling young age of thirty-two. She felt secure in God's timing and so had left questions such as marriage and family in his hands. Although lately, she had been aware of the fact that her biological clock was running. She couldn't wait forever if she were to have the children she had always dreamed of having. And now . . .

She settled back in the cushions with a sigh and closed her eyes. In her euphoric state she could imagine herself anywhere—but she didn't want to be anywhere else, only where Gavin was.

And then her prince was before her, handing her a cup of tea with a plate of cakes and tiny finger sandwiches. As he relaxed his long form on the couch beside her, Elizabeth wondered just how closely life repeated art. "Where did you go to college—or, I guess you'd say university?"

"Oxford," he replied around the outside of a tea sandwich.

"Wimsey's Balliol?"

"Absolutely."

If she hadn't been holding a teacup she would have applauded. "Perfect! I don't suppose you collect rare manuscripts, too?"

"I collect books, period. Nothing in Latin quattrocento, I'm afraid. Just books, anything that takes my fancy."

"Cricket?" She was fascinated to learn how far the parallels to her fictional heroes extended.

"What you would call 'sandlot baseball' we call 'country house cricket.' I've done a bit, but nothing in the style of Raffles' All-England Bowling, I'm afraid."

"Raffles?"

"Oh, haven't you read him? An Edwardian rogue that steals from the rich and gives to the poor—except he's the poor he gives to."

Elizabeth stared. "You mean, he's the hero?"

Gavin nodded. "Clever fellow. Fun reading."

Elizabeth did not want to start an argument by going into her strongly held opinions regarding stories upholding the notion that crime did pay, so she turned her attention to the refreshments. "Mmm, aren't these cream cheese and walnut sandwiches good!"

They continued chatting, chiefly about their families: Her younger twin brother and sister— "He's working on a ranch, and she'll graduate from college this spring"; his older sister who was married to a London chemist and had two children—"It must be handy for a thriller writer to have a pharmacologist in the family, ready reference to anything you need to know about poisons or drugs?"

"Absolutely, I call on George's expertise frequently. Finished?" He took the empty cup from her hand. "Would you care to walk around the lake a bit, if it isn't too cold?"

"Some fresh air would be great. I haven't been outside since we arrived. I hope we're all through with that storm business. But then, early spring in the Rockies, you never know."

He held the door for her, and they went out onto the wooden veranda that ran around two sides of the Lake Lounge room then led to a nar-

row footpath encircling the water. The lake was
actually the quarry that had supplied the pink
and gray stone for the original castle, the quarry
having since been filled with water. On the castle side, the path was a gentle trail through
small trees—but across the lake, the way led
high above the sheer face of the rock wall.

Sir Gavin took her hand and slipped it through
his arm as they walked close together on the narrow path. At frequent intervals along the many
footpaths that jigsawed over the mountain, tiny
wooden gazebos were provided for the hikers' rest
or the photographers' interest. Gavin led her into
one of these that sat right by the edge of the still
lake. The sun was bright but cold, and the craggy
chunks of the granite cliff that reflected on the surface of the lake made even the water seem hard.
Elizabeth shivered.

Gavin slipped his arm around her, providing
a warm haven in contrast to the hard, cold environment around them. His wool gabardine
jacket was smooth and soft, and the man inside
it was warm as he pulled Elizabeth to him.

She held her breath, wanting the moment to
last forever. That first kiss provided all the assurance she needed that she was right. They were
Gavin and Elizabeth, at once more and less
than all her dreams.

They were all lovers of all times sharing the
sweetness and intensity of the first meeting of
lips. At the same time they were the most per-

49

sonal and essential parts of their own being, meeting and sharing as only they could. They were all universal love standing strong against all universal hatred, and yet they were their most individual selves meeting as only they could meet in the absolute privacy of the moment. Cinderella and her prince, Romeo and Juliet, Fred Astaire and Ginger Rogers, Peter Wimsey and Harriet Vane, Gavin Kendall and Elizabeth Allerton . . . a continuum of the symbolic essence of love . . . a beacon to prove that fairy tales could come true.

The rest of the evening Elizabeth hardly touched ground. The uneven spots in the old corridors put her in no danger of tripping; she merely floated over them. For dinner she wore the black silk skirt her sister, a home ec major, had designed for her, its six gores fitting slimly to below the knees, then flaring gracefully just above her ankles. Her white draped blouse was made of alternate rows of satin ribbon and lace and the long black feather that curved away from her smooth cap of hair looked like something out of an Edward Gorey illustration.

Sir Gavin assured all the enthusiastic diners at the Blithe Spirit table that the veal and mushroom pie in pastry crust, accompanied by an assortment of vegetables, was typical English fare—especially the deliciously tart gooseberry fool that arrived for dessert. Elizabeth ate portions of everything the waiter placed before her,

smiled and nodded at all the theories being pro-
pounded by the amateur sleuths around the
table, and even chatted briefly with Richard,
whom she hadn't seen since before tea. But all
the time she was moving in a dream—a dream
within a dream—as the romance of a mystery
week had turned into the romance of her life.

She and Gavin sat long over their after-dinner
tea. It wasn't until the dining room was almost
empty and the fire had burned low on the grate
that they rose to walk slowly to the parlor
where old mystery movies, set in the thirties,
were shown in the evenings. Tonight's choice
was a romantic mystery set in the Mediterranean with a sunny sky and bright blue sea as
backdrop for a honeymooning couple whose
love was almost torn apart by murder, suspicions, and accusations.

But Elizabeth didn't see the actress on the
screen; she saw herself. When the heroine held her
new husband in her arms on the balcony of their
honeymoon suite and said, "Oh, Randolph . . . all
my life I've been groping—homeless—but now
I've found you. I am home," silent tears made little splotches on Elizabeth's silk skirt, and she
ached to take the man beside her into her arms.

Black clouds roiled across the Mediterranean
sky, covering the gold, but she ran on up the
beach. She must find him, find him and warn
him. . . .

A loud crash brought Elizabeth sitting upright in bed. As her breathing slowed and her ragged nerves calmed, she realized her dreams had been a continuation of the movie. Her sleep-clouded brain was still trying to figure out whether the explosion that woke her was the dream's gathering storm or the villain's gun when she realized it was the rumble of a real thunderstorm. The smoke she was smelling was not from a fantasy revolver, either, but was coming from the fireplace in the parlor just down the hall. She got up, slipped into her clothes and went out to see what in the world Richard was up to at this hour.

"Richard! you look awful!" She stood in the doorway, unable to believe that the man who at dinner had been such a perfection of sleek polish in his tuxedo and starched wing-tipped shirt was now such a rumple of tousled hair, wrinkled cords and sweater, and dark-circled, haunted-looking eyes.

He ran his fingers through his hair, disheveling it even more, if possible. "Elizabeth, I'm sorry, I didn't mean to waken you—"

"You didn't, it was the thunder. It shook the whole place and jarred me upright in bed. What are you doing? Are you sick?"

"No. That is, I couldn't sleep. Things on my mind, I guess." He slumped back on the sofa, the flickering fireplace making weird shadows dance across his gaunt face.

Elizabeth crossed the room and curled up on

the opposite end of the sofa. "Want to talk about it?"

"I don't know. I've never been much into the small group sharing thing . . . but maybe . . . "

Elizabeth waited quietly. He could make up his own mind, and whatever he decided was all right with her. If he wanted to talk, though, she was available.

"I guess it's all the talk about death, and then the honeymoon movie tonight . . . even the actress who played Gloria last night had an uncanny resemblance to Mary."

Elizabeth caught her breath. Mary . . . Richard's wife. "Richard, you've never talked about her. I didn't even have any idea what she looked like."

"No." He leaned forward, elbows on knees, head in hands, shoulders slumped. "At first it hurt too much. After a while, I'd worked through it, and there wasn't any need, or anyone I really wanted to talk to. Then you came into my life—"

Ignoring his last words, Elizabeth said quickly, "What did Mary die of?"

"Abruptio placentae. She was eight months pregnant. The placenta pulled away from the uterus. She had terrible cramps, and I rushed her to the hospital. They should have been able to save her or the baby, but the hemorrhaging was too severe, and there was blood poisoning."

Elizabeth was silent, watching the grotesque

shadows from the fire dance before them like the souls of the Wilis—those legendary souls of sad and unfulfilled young girls who died before their wedding.

"It was a little girl."

Elizabeth opened her arms, and he turned into them. She knew it had happened four years ago, after they had been married three years. But that was all she had known until this moment. She had no idea that all this time Richard had carried such an unremitting ache inside him. She had no idea that it had been a double loss, wife and child. A daughter. She would be in kindergarten now. Would she have been blond like her mother or darker like her father? She looked at the head of the man she held in her arms, and it seemed that for the first time, she really saw him. Not the professor, not the academic brain, not the well-organized automaton, but a man—a warm, emotional human being with an agonizing need for another human being.

She wished she could be the one to fill his need. If she hadn't met Gavin, if she hadn't experienced the difference in her feelings, perhaps . . .

Well, if she wasn't the right person, someone else would be. Someone as absolutely right for Richard as Gavin was for her. Anita, perhaps? She certainly showed every sign of being willing. All right, Elizabeth decided, she would do everything she could to encourage their relationship.

5

Wednesday

The next morning, ready for breakfast in his camel-hair blazer, ivory slacks, and red-and-gold-paisley ascot, no one would have guessed the well-buried pain Richard had revealed to Elizabeth. He smiled at her as she came into the sitting room. "The college must be overpaying you. That's your third new outfit in as many days."

"Fourth, actually." She twirled around, sending the circular skirt of her winter white dress swirling about her calves, then rearranged the loops of gold chains in the folds of the cowl neckline. "That's the result of careful reading of those catalogs you're always giving me such a bad time about. And don't worry about my being overpaid. They couldn't possibly pay me what I'm worth."

Elizabeth enjoyed knowing they looked good together as they descended the stairs. The others seemed to be enjoying them, too. A middle-aged lady from another team greeted them in the dining room. "Your costumes are simply beautiful—both of you. If they gave a prize for best costumes, you'd win."

Elizabeth gave her a beaming thank-you, and they crossed the wooden floor to their table, where all heads were bent toward Irene, who was explaining her theory identifying Millie as the murderer.

Gavin joined them just as the waiter was serving a large platter of a smoked fish and rice dish. "Oh, good show—kedgeree."

"So this is kedgeree!" Elizabeth took a heaping spoonful, "I always wondered; Agatha Christie's Tommy was forever talking about it."

Gavin picked up a glass of tomato juice. "To Tommy, kedgeree . . . ," He lowered his voice and looked at Elizabeth, "and to you."

Elizabeth laughed and raised her glass. Only when she was drinking did the thought occur to her that the last person this man had toasted had been Gloria Glitz.

Before any ironies could take hold, Weldon Stark turned everyone's attention to the front of the room, where he was holding up a newspaper and a magazine. "Ladies and gentlemen, I bring you good news and greetings from His Majesty's Royal Mail. The courageous postman has braved the heavy storms still battering the moors and making the roads impassable to all but the most lionhearted to deliver a supply of reading material for your entertainment and edification." A round of applause interrupted him. "Copies of these enlightening publications have been distributed to all the lounge areas. Happy reading."

"New clues!" Evan Johnson was on his feet, closely followed by his sister.

"Come on, we can take our coffee with us!" Irene signaled the waiter for a refill.

"What a beautiful jacket, Richard. And that red silk pocket handkerchief is a marvelous touch." Elizabeth smiled as she watched Anita take charge of Richard. It didn't appear as if she would need to do much assisting to get a companion for Richard.

The library was well supplied with the mock-up material. Half of the team selected copies of the *Times* for March 15, 1933, and the others settled into chairs with similarly dated issues of *Punch*.

"Oh dear, the Prince of Wales is still seeing that horrible American woman," Helen Johnson remarked, looking up from her magazine. "There's going to be trouble over that yet."

Irene agreed. "I think so, too. It's enough to make one feel he should apologize for being American."

"I think Mrs. Simpson's a classy lady," Benton teased his daughter. "Probably worth having a row over."

"Oh, but look at the next article!" Anita

turned her magazine to display a full-page photo of Gloria Glitz.

Pages rustled as all the *Punch* readers scrambled after the bait. "Ah-ha!" Irene noted with glee. "This says she was behind on her rate payments—that's what we call taxes."

Questions and theories buzzed around the room.

"Do you suppose she was short of money?"

"If so, why didn't Nigel take care of it?"

"Maybe she committed suicide to avoid the scandal."

"Just when she was about to get her hands on all of Sir Linden's money?"

"Maybe he killed her to keep her hands off his money," Evan speculated.

"Then why did he propose to her, dummy?" Cathy shot back, and Evan made a face at his sister.

"Is there anything about it in the *Times?*" Helen asked, glancing at Bill.

"I don't see anything about that, but here's an article about the Foreign Office fearing a security leak."

"Does it name Brian?"

"Doesn't name anybody, but it says they fear top operators may be involved. Hmmm, one wonders . . . "

"I wonder which things are actual news stories from '33 and which things are plants for the game," Anita said.

"They did them well, didn't they?" Helen agreed. "They must have printing facilities right here at the hotel, because I don't think the landslide has been cleared yet."

"Oh, these were probably done a week ago. But listen to this item in the gossip column!" Cathy exclaimed, then read: "'All ears in the West End are strained to catch the name of the perennial understudy who is in love with the man her leading lady is to wed.'"

"But could that mean Gloria and Linden? Their engagement hadn't been announced yet."

"Don't worry, Gertie Gossip would have had the scoop on that long before it was official."

"So Susie was in love with Linden. Now there's a motive," Irene said thoughtfully.

"Why isn't there anything in here about the murder?"

"These are Monday's papers—the storm has slowed down communications."

"Well, if the mail could get through, you'd think Scotland Yard could."

"They don't need Scotland Yard, they've got us," Evan said with a grin.

Anita looked at him and shrugged. "I still think she just choked—you don't need Scotland Yard for a natural death."

"Seems everyone had a motive for killing her, though," Irene mused.

"Oh!" Cathy gave a shrill shriek. Everyone

looked at her. "Maybe that's it! Maybe they all did it—like *Murder on the Orient Express!*"

"Yeah!" Everyone leaned forward.

"Why?" Richard asked.

Everyone sat back, like deflating balloons.

After a moment the team continued reading and chatting, commenting on interesting tidbits of genuine period events and the planted articles. Elizabeth turned to the library shelves behind her. They were well stocked with reading material to appeal to people attending a mystery week: Wilkie Collins, The Complete Sherlock Holmes, Ngaio Marsh, Josephine Tey . . . mysteries, thrillers, whodunits. Then there was a shelf of technical books on forensic toxicology and crime statistics, including *A Medicolegal Investigation of Death,* and *Bloodstain Pattern Interpretation*. But Elizabeth's fancy was taken by a stack of old magazines. She blew the dust off of an issue of *Time* and began turning the pages. She smiled to see how little some things changed. The romance of another Prince of Wales was in the news. An even older issue brought a wave of nostalgia with a rundown on the new TV shows for the season. Names that had been stellar at that moment were now all but forgotten. She shook her head over the impermanence of popularity and picked up another magazine.

Oh my goodness, she thought as she skimmed the list of best-sellers. *How time flies.* She turned to the cover—the date was years ago. Amazing.

It seemed those books had always existed, like
Mother Goose or Peter Rabbit. And here was
a review of a new biography of Agatha
Christie . . .

Elizabeth was now completely lost to the
chatter around her. Sneezing at the dust, she
picked up another magazine with a five-year-old
dateline, then gasped at her good fortune. Here
was a review of *Who Doth Murder Sleep?* and a
picture of the author, looking only slightly
younger than he did at breakfast this morning.
The photograph was of him (just plain Gavin
Kendall, since he hadn't yet received his knighthood) escorting the actress Margo Lovell to a
West End gala. Elizabeth stared at the picture as
if the figures had begun to move. She hadn't
realized how glamorous his life undoubtedly
was—how far-removed his world was from hers.
Because they read the same books, liked the
same food, and her heart turned handsprings at
the merest thought of Gavin, she hadn't considered the differences between them. Could the
distances of cultural and social background be
spanned by love? For the first time since Sir
Gavin Kendall bowed over her hand as a romantic hero, shadows of doubt and fear touched
her heart and made her shiver.

To help clear her thoughts, she focused on
the review below the picture: "This spine-tin-
gling thriller is a totally new style for the writer
whose previous mysteries have been no more

than charming period pieces. Gavin Kendall has at last given us full-fleshed characters caught in fast-paced action and cliff-hanging suspense. . . . There are already rumors that if the international accolades continue to mount, a knighthood could be in the offing. In the meantime, we look forward to more books in this vein from a writer who has suddenly hit his stride . . . "

"See, I knew it was Suzanna—jealousy will do it every time."

"That's a weaker motive than national security. Not only that, but Brian's whole career was on the line as well."

The talk in the room penetrated her consciousness as Elizabeth looked through another stack of red-bordered magazines to see if she could find a review of Gavin's more recent books.

"Well, if you want to talk about careers, look at Nigel Cass—he's obviously mismanaged Gloria's business affairs, if not outright stolen from her. And don't forget, the thing happened in his home. He'd have far more opportunity than anyone else."

"Which is precisely why he wouldn't do it—it would be too obvious to murder his own guest."

"Oh, I don't know—Macbeth did."

"Yeah, and he didn't get away with it, either."

"Macbeth tried to put the blame on the servants and then killed them all before they could talk. And speaking of servants, I think Millie knows more than she's telling."

A musical chime turned everyone's attention to the clock on the mantle.

"Noon already?"

"We just ate."

"The food here is incredible."

A wail from Irene made everyone laugh as they moved toward the dining room. "And I have a Weight Watchers meeting a week from tonight!"

Elizabeth joined the group excitedly. She couldn't wait to tell Gavin about the article she had found about him.

" . . . and they gave you more space than Agatha Christie's biography."

With his British reserve, Gavin seemed less pleased about her accolades than she had expected, so she changed the subject slightly, "I looked for a review of your more recent books, but I didn't find anything. Stark said the first night of this week that you gave him the plot for this mystery. It's such a good one, why didn't you ever use it yourself? Or did you? I'm afraid I haven't read all of your books."

Gavin shrugged and finished a bite of his shrimp salad. "Thank goodness they serve American lunches here—you'd never get salads like this in England. And they do a much better job of cooking the vegetables here, too."

Elizabeth laughed. "Yes, just because 'there'll always be an England' is no reason to cook the vegetables to death."

"Precisely my point." Gavin took another bite of salad, so he was chewing again when Elizabeth returned to the subject of the mystery plot.

He shook his head and wiped his mouth with his napkin. "No, I never used it. It's fine for a game like this—really a lot of fun—but it would never do for a book. Much too thin and contrived. Wouldn't be believable at all. Of course, I don't know if Stark is going to use the ending I suggested. He's already made several changes to fit the situation. As for my books, well, they are all in the shop downstairs. As well as Stark's and a good selection of the classics: Christie, Sayers, Margery Allingham—"

But the magazine article was still foremost in Elizabeth's mind, and she didn't take the offer to discuss other mystery writers. "The picture of you with Margo Lovell was stunning. Is she still acting? I haven't heard anything about her for years."

"A most startling event has just been discovered—" Weldon Stark's agitated voice caught everyone's attention, and Gavin's answer to Elizabeth's question was lost. "Millie Maeda has disappeared. We fear foul play as the kitchen shows signs of struggle, including her apron having been ripped off." He held up a white ruffled apron with the strings still tied, but pulled apart at the side.

"We have it on the best of authority that no abductor would be so foolish as to hide his vic-

tim in a guest's room, but with that as the only
off-limits, there is a ten-point bonus for the
team who finds Millie—or her body," he con-
cluded darkly.

"Oh, wow! A manhunt!" Evan's eyes glowed
with excitement.

"That's womanhunt," Cathy reminded her
brother.

"Uh-ho, Millie knew too much—do you suppose it was that argument she overheard?" It
seemed that Irene played the whole game on
the edge of her chair.

"It looks bad for Nigel," Bill Johnson agreed.

"Maybe it wasn't that at all." Helen frowned
thoughtfully. "Maybe the poison was in the
soup, but Millie didn't put it there, and the
murderer is afraid she'll figure out who did."

"It would be interesting to know who visited
the kitchen before dinner. Let's try to find out
next time we interview witnesses."

"Shall we retire to the library to get organized?" Richard held Elizabeth's chair for her.

As soon as they were in their meeting room
Richard continued, "There are four floors, so I
suggest we work in four teams."

Elizabeth knew a moment of secret delight as
Anita started to volunteer to work with Richard, but her delight turned to dismay when
Irene invited Anita to work with Benton and
herself. There was nothing Anita could do but
agree gracefully.

Most of the searching activity was centered in the lounge rooms and public areas on the first two floors, so the fourth floor was comparatively quiet for Elizabeth and Richard.

Elizabeth wanted to talk to him about the night before, but wasn't sure how to approach the subject: "Did you sleep all right?" "How are you today?" "That was a quite a storm we had last night." None of the subtle approaches seemed right. Then she knew.

"Thank you for sharing with me last night, Richard," she said quietly.

He gave a sardonic little half-smile. "That's tactful of you. I was about to apologize for the melodrama."

"Oh, no! Please don't think that. I felt honored. You know, I never knew—," she interrupted herself to open a linen closet and make sure there could be no body tucked behind the stacks of sheets, "—about the baby." She laid her hand on his arm for the briefest moment.

He walked on down the hall. "In a way that was the hardest part. I—we—had looked forward so to raising children." He stopped before a door labeled "Men," and pointed her to the one marked "Women."

"I'll meet you back out here," he said.

Elizabeth walked in without the slightest hesitation and checked the stalls, under the sinks, behind the shower curtain. Nothing. When there was only one place left to check, Elizabeth paused. This was really silly. So what if Millie were lying in the bathtub? Why should that frighten her? It was all just playacting. But this extended role-playing got ahold of you so. Sometimes it was hard to separate reality from fantasy.

She took a deep breath and yanked the bath door open. Weak laughter accompanied her relief at finding the tub empty. With a firm vow to be more sensible in the future, she went out to meet Richard.

"No luck?" he asked.

"I'll have to admit I considered that lucky."

"Is that first night still bothering you?"

"No, of course not." Then she thought of Richard's open honesty to her. "Well, some. Shall we just say I'm a little shy when it comes to meeting bodies in bathtubs?"

One of the uneven floorboards caught her foot, and she started to stumble, but Richard caught her arm. "Thanks," she said, "I have all the bumps memorized at our end of the hall." She was now on firm footing, but Richard still held her arm.

And he continued to hold it even when the small alcove at the end of the dim hall proved empty and they had turned to search the other direction.

"We were talking about children," Elizabeth prompted.

Richard nodded. "Yes, we were." He was

quiet so long Elizabeth thought the conversation must be over. Then he said, "I think the thing I always looked forward to most was teaching them things. By the time I get students in college, most of them are either all confused or overconfident. The joy of having a fresh, inquiring, young mind to guide, to show the world, to teach about God—" he stopped.

"It isn't too late, you know. You can still have children. You'll meet somebody."

The pressure of his hand increased on her arm. "I thought I had." The infinite sadness in his voice made her choke.

Then another team came around the corner from the south corridor. "Any luck?" they called.

Richard replied to them, "We searched that direction. Didn't find anything."

"Let's go downstairs." The team went into a huddle.

"We should check that hall, maybe they missed something," someone suggested.

"Isn't there an attic to this place?"

"Look for trapdoors."

Elizabeth and Richard walked on until she noticed something in the wainscoting. "Look! They just said trapdoors, and here one is—now I remember noticing it earlier."

Richard tapped at the section of paneling surrounded by a narrow molding. A hollow sound answered him. "You're right. It probably goes to a crawl space that leads to heating pipes, wiring, plumbing—whatever servicemen might need to get to." He took a key out of his pocket and pried at the molding. The panel wrenched loose from the wall.

Elizabeth bent over and peered into the black space. "If this really were a house in England I'd say that was a priest hole. What a perfect place to hide a body."

"Don't suppose you packed a flashlight?"

"No. And it's sure to be filthy in there—with us both wearing white." She thought for a moment. "Oh, there are candles in those sconces on the wall by the fireplace. I'll be right back." She sped down the corridor to her room, then turned and called back, "Don't leave that spot—we found it, I want the points."

In a few minutes, she was back. Richard held the flickering flame in the hole. Even with the little they could see from the tiny light, it didn't take long for their disappointment to register. There was no body curled in the doorway, and the presence of cobwebs hanging from the pipes made clear the futility of crawling behind the walls in either direction.

Richard puffed out the candle and pushed the paneling back into place. "Well, so much for that brilliant idea."

"But there must be others. I'll bet every corridor has one of those for repair access."

"Right, keep watching for them, and we'll check 'em out."

They turned off the main passage into their own, which still was largely unoccupied. Elizabeth looked around thoughtfully. "They said no guests' rooms, but empty ones ought to be fair game." She tried a door across the hall just down from hers. "Locked. Do you suppose we could pick it?"

"Why not just ask the desk for a key?"

Elizabeth laughed. "What logic! I would never have thought of anything so simple—my mind was full of bent hairpins, nail files, credit cards—"

"Credit cards?"

"Sure. It's supposed to be great for getting into rooms—just slide it down the crack between door and casing and trip the lock mechanism."

Richard shook his head. "What a life of crime you must have led before I met you. Reading thrillers is more degrading than reading catalogs."

"Wrong. I learned that little gem from a catalog—they were advertising a device you can put on your locks to prevent them being picked that way."

Richard backed away, holding up his hands. "I don't want to hear any more. You guard our territory. I'll be right back with a key."

In less time than she could have imagined, he was back, displaying a brass key on the palm of his hand. "They said it should do all the doors in this wing. Ours are the only ones occupied."

"I'm really impressed. You went up and down

three flights of stairs in about three minutes, and you're not even winded." She took the key from his hand and unlocked the first door.

"Clean living, good conditioning," Richard said with a note of satisfaction as he followed her into the room.

"Ugh, I'm glad they didn't put us in here." Elizabeth held her nose at the musty smell from the long-closed room. She flicked a piece of curling wallpaper. "No wonder they plan to redecorate."

A careful search behind and under the furniture—which was pushed to the center of the room—in the closet and bathroom, and behind the curtains, revealed no trussed and gagged Millie. Nor did they find her in any of the rooms on that side of the hall.

They crossed the hall and began working back toward their room. "The rooms on this side all have balconies," Elizabeth noted. "That's something else to check." Elizabeth pulled the dusty drapes open to let some light in. "Brr, it's cold. If they put her in one of these rooms, I hope they put a coat on her."

They searched carefully, but found nothing. "Oh, phooey! And I thought we had such a clever idea. Someone probably found her an hour ago downstairs while we're still grubbing around up here."

"Well, there's only one room left, then we

can go get some tea." Richard fit the key into the door of the room next to his.

"I thought it was getting close to tea time. I'm hungry. It doesn't—"

Richard stopped so abruptly Elizabeth banged into him. "Shh, someone is taking a nap in here." He began backing out of the dark room.

At the door Elizabeth stopped and gave his back a shove forward. "Idiot! That must be Millie! No one's staying in here." She sidestepped Richard and crossed the room to open the drapes. "My, but it smells musty in here."

Elizabeth turned back just as Richard pulled the blankets off the form on the bed. One hand flew to her mouth to stifle her gasp. "It . . . it's that actor . . . the one in my room the first night!"

Elizabeth held her breath while Richard felt the limp wrist, then unbuttoned the man's shirt and laid a hand on his chest. Finally Richard looked at her, his face grim.

"I'm afraid he's not acting now."

6

Elizabeth didn't faint this time, but once back in her sitting room, she huddled in the corner of the sofa, wrapped in a blanket, and did her best to stop shivering. Dr. Pearsall and the hotel manager, Mr. Hamlin, arrived promptly at Richard's summons.

"Where is the patient?" Dr. Pearsall was already putting his stethoscope in his ears.

Elizabeth rose to go to the next room with the others, but Richard held out a restraining hand. "Don't you think you should wait here?"

She shook her head firmly, and Richard gave way. In the room, however, Elizabeth sat where she could watch the men work without being obliged to look at the body.

"I don't understand this at all." The manager paced around the small room. "No one is registered for this room, and with our security, it's not possible for a vagrant to slip in."

73

Dr. Pearsall examined the Harris tweed jacket with leather elbow patches. "I don't think he was a bum; his clothes are good quality." He put his hand in each pocket. "No ID, nothing—not a coin or a piece of string or anything."

Elizabeth pushed the blanket back from her shoulders and spoke for the first time since entering the room. "But he must have been staying in here because the room is warm. The unoccupied ones were icy."

Mr. Hamlin shook his head. "No, the heat in this room is controlled by the thermostat in the room next door. It's a crazy system, one of the things we plan to fix when we remodel. No two people ever want their rooms the same temperature—somebody always complains."

He began pacing again. "This is most awkward. With the landslide business we could have absolute panic if the guests learn they're stranded here with a live corpse."

Elizabeth gave a nervous giggle.

"Oh, I meant a real corpse, of course. This hotel has built a nationwide reputation with our mystery weeks—I don't want anything to put a damper on it. Do you have any idea yet what he died of, Doc?"

Dr. Pearsall wiped his forehead. "The way he's lying and all, looks like he just went to sleep and didn't wake up. I mean, there aren't any visible signs of any problems. But this is my first time trying to determine such a thing, you know—

other than with the cadavers in med school, of course."

"A man lies down in all his clothes for a nap in an unoccupied room that's supposed to be locked, and decides not to wake up?" Richard's voice held more than a hint of scorn.

"I agree it sounds preposterous," the doctor said, although Mr. Hamlin looked as if he'd be happy to let the matter drop right there. "Of course, what we need are lab facilities. The coroner's autopsy will tell us everything we need to know."

"That's great. And how do you propose to get the . . . er, body to the coroner?" The manager faced the doctor.

Richard saved the uncomfortable doctor from having to answer the unanswerable. "Do you have any idea how long he's been dead?"

Dr. Pearsall turned back to his patient, wiggled the man's slack jaw and bent the fingers on his left hand back and forth. "No sign of rigor mortis setting in yet, so it can't have been long, two or three hours." He put his hand on the pale forehead. "Body temp gone, though. Say three hours."

Everyone looked at their watches. "Right after lunch," Elizabeth said.

"Yeah, that's about right. One o'clock or so, in very general terms, you understand. Without actual tests—" the doctor hedged, but Elizabeth wasn't listening. She and Richard had been on this floor by one-thirty. There had been a few members of other teams poking around, but had she noticed anyone in this hall? Maybe she had seen the man and thought he was another player? She wished she could remember something helpful.

"Best to leave him here until we can get him to the proper facilities?" Dr. Pearsall asked.

"Yes. By all means." It was clear Mr. Hamlin didn't want any corpses carried through his hotel in broad daylight. "And we'll keep this unfortunate event just between those of us in this room— no need to worry the others. Right?"

"Worry us about what?" A jaunty voice made them all turn to the doorway. "I say Elizabeth, have I been stood up for tea?"

"Oh, Gavin, I'm sorry. I forgot. We found this . . . "

At her gesture toward the bed Gavin came further into the room, putting his glass in his eye just as Hercule Poirot would have. "You don't mean he's really copped it this time?"

"What? You know him?" The manager showed signs of relief.

"Not exactly. We only met once. But he is— was—one of the actors."

"Get Stark up here!" The manager looked around for a telephone, then realized there wasn't one in the room.

"Shall we move next door? The parlor is more

comfortable," Richard suggested, then led the way.

"Yes, yes. Glad you find it so. The tower rooms really are quite nice." Mr. Hamlin spoke like a recording.

Weldon Stark answered his summons promptly, but his comments only added to the confusion. "No, I've never seen him before. What made you think he was part of my cast?"

"That's what he told me," Gavin said from where he sat on the sofa beside Elizabeth.

"He told you? When?"

Elizabeth spoke up. "The first night. After the landslide. He was in my bathtub. Scared me to death, but he told Gavin it was just part of the script."

"That's right." Gavin took up her story. "But after the stunt went so awry, scaring Elizabeth so badly, I told him to tell you we'd just have to scrub that bit."

Weldon Stark pushed his glasses up on his nose. "Well, he was lying. He was definitely not part of my cast. There was nothing like that in the scenario."

"Quick thinking on his part," Richard said.

"But if he wasn't part of the play, what was he doing in my room?" Elizabeth's hand went to her throat, her dark eyes were wide and round.

"Trying to shelter from the storm?"

"A journalist looking for a backstairs story?"

The suggestions seemed weak, but Elizabeth didn't like the alternative that occurred to her— he had chosen a woman's room in an isolated part of the hotel . . .

But Mr. Hamlin's mind was working in another direction. "Miss Allerton, do you have anything of value with you? Jewelry, perhaps?"

Elizabeth laughed. "I've never owned anything worth stealing. Most of the things I brought this week are rented. Oh, except my grandmother's pearl brooch, which I wore the first night—" She broke off abruptly, then rushed to her room and yanked open the top dresser drawer. Nothing had been touched.

When she returned, smiling with relief, Gavin was questioning Richard, "Do you have anything someone might want to steal—old books or manuscripts with you? Anything in your research notes?"

Richard made a wry face. "I only wish I did."

"Well," Gavin said, "it seems clear that whatever he was up to, it was no good. Why else would he be so careful not to carry any identification?"

"The only thing to do is to leave him right where he is until we can contact the authorities in a day or two. Whatever he was doing, he's no danger to anyone now." The manager turned to Stark. "I suggest you go right ahead with your program as if nothing happened. We all agreed before you came that it would be best to say nothing to alarm the other guests."

They hadn't exactly agreed earlier, but everyone seemed in agreement now. As the others were leaving, Gavin turned to Elizabeth. "Tea time is over in the lounge, but shall I order you some from the kitchen?"

Elizabeth laughed. "If chicken soup is Jewish penicillin, tea must be British Valium. But it's not such a bad idea. I'll take a cup, nice and strong with lots of milk, please."

"Something stronger for you?" he asked, looking at Richard.

"No. Thanks. Tea for me, too."

Since the hotel offered no room service, Gavin departed for the kitchen. Richard turned to Elizabeth and put his arms around her comfortingly. "Are you all right?"

She gave a little choked laugh and nodded, her head rubbing against his chest. "Yes, I'm fine. Really. Strange isn't it, but I was more upset when he was acting than when it was for real."

"Do you want to move to another room?"

"No, not at all. But thank you for asking, Richard, that's very thoughtful of you." Who would have guessed Richard would be so sensitive? She didn't want to move to another room, and neither did she want to move from the comfort of his arms at the moment. "What I would like is to pray together. Do you suppose

that poor man ever heard the gospel? He probably didn't have any idea he was going to die—
and then suddenly . . . " She shivered, and
Richard held her tighter.

She felt his lips move before she heard his
voice. "Our Father, in the midst of life we are in
death. From whom may we seek comfort but
from thee? Though we walk through the valley
of the shadow of death, we will fear no evil, for
you are with us, your rod and your staff they
comfort us."

He paused, and she wondered if she should
say amen. Then he continued. "We meekly
beseech you, Father, to raise us from the death
of sin unto the life of righteousness; that, when
we depart this life, we may rest in you.

"And God of mercy, we ask your mercy for the
soul of this man that now stands before you.
Glory be to the Father, and to the Son, and to
the Holy Ghost: As it was in the beginning, is
now, and ever shall be: world without end.
Amen."

Elizabeth didn't move, she just stood there
silently, letting the strength and magnificence of
those words sink into her soul: "When we depart
this life, we may rest in you . . . "

She suddenly felt perfectly at rest. "That was
beautiful, Richard."

"I memorized that years ago for its beauty and
comfort—four years ago to be exact. It's hard to

80

beat the *Book of Common Prayer* for the crisis moments of life."

"Here, sit down now." He led her to the sofa. "I'll light the fire. You still feel cold."

The maid had relaid the fire that morning, so it was only a matter of seconds until a crackling blaze was warming the room. Richard sat beside her.

She turned to him. "Wouldn't it be awful if that really were the end? What if that was all there was to life, just to end up lying there like that man? If there were no hope—just a limp, cold, empty body?"

"Yes . . . " Richard's thought hung in midair. "And so?"

He shrugged. "Nothing really new, but it's a powerful reminder of how fragile life is. I mean, that poor fellow may have been sick, but he probably had no idea his end was so near."

"Mmm." She nodded. "One doesn't think about it much. I mean, Saint Paul said that if we have hope in this life only, we are most miserable. But I've never agreed. I always thought the joy of God's presence and daily guidance were quite enough. Oh, of course, I believed in eternal life and all that, but it just wasn't that important to me . . . but now that I've actually seen death—it's—it's very unsettling."

"You've never seen it before?"

"Well, I've been to funerals, of course, with music and flowers, and the dear departed in

81

folds of white satin—but this was something altogether different. It happened right there, maybe while we were just down the hall . . . "

Richard moved closer and put his arm around her, then pulled away when he heard Gavin at the door. Soon they were all sipping cups of rich, hot tea and hungrily consuming chocolate cookies that Gavin insisted on calling biscuits, and laughing at Gavin's comic relief: "Frightfully awkward, that blighter popping off like that right next door. I mean, it's not done, positively not done. It creates such a tiresome mess, not letting anyone know who you are or what you're doing. Simply too mystery-making. I mean, really."

Elizabeth laughed so hard she had to set her cup down. "You do that so well, Gavin! And what a relief to laugh after all that intensity." They were all quiet a moment as the fire crackled cheerfully. "Really, though, I would love to know more about that poor man. Why he turned to a life of crime—if he was a criminal, that is."

"If not criminal, certainly something suspicious." Gavin refilled Elizabeth's cup. "But it will most likely be cleared up quickly enough when the police get here. I expect he was a local who just walked up the mountain from Hidden Glenn. Hotel security would prevent anyone unregistered from driving up, but they can't patrol the whole mountain for hikers."

"Yes." Richard laid his crumpled napkin on the tray and leaned back. "That would explain his not having a billfold. He wouldn't need it for a walk in the country."

"But it's hardly been hiking weather since we got here," Elizabeth objected. "And if he was just passing by, why would he make up that elaborate lie the first night?"

Gavin shrugged. "Maybe to keep from getting thrown out in the storm. He knew he couldn't pay for a room."

Elizabeth shook her head. "You're nice guys to look for answers that leave him an honest man, but I'm afraid he was up to no good. I mean, I don't have anything of much value, but one or two of the teams are all Texans, and that may mean oil money. I'll bet their jewelry isn't rented from the costume shop."

Richard took the empty cup from her hands and set it down. "If some of the glitter I saw at dinner last night was real, it would certainly be enough to attract a jewel thief."

"Dinner!" The word brought Gavin to his feet. "I say, there's just time to change. Leave all that." He motioned to the tea tray. "The maid will get it later."

At first Elizabeth was uncomfortable entering the buzzing dining room—she felt that one glance at her would give the whole secret away—but after two minutes of listening to the excited chatter around the table, she relaxed. "Oh, was Millie found? We got . . . er, sidetracked."

As usual, Irene was the first to pick up her line. "The Circle found her. Guess what? She was right here in the dining room all the time— bound and gagged and hidden under the salad bar."

Elizabeth looked at the long table in the center of the room with the gold tablecloth hanging in precise folds to the floor. "What a great place! Everyone in the room passed within inches of her! I love it! Did she see her abductor?"

"Stark announced that she was too shaken by the experience to be interviewed right then. He said Dr. Pearsall would give her a sedative, and she would be available for questioning in the morning after breakfast."

"They'd better all be available." Evan patted the notebook beside his plate. "I've got plenty of questions that need answering."

Elizabeth smiled at his intensity. "Evan, I think we may be witnessing the birth of a new Sherlock Holmes."

Evan's sister cut in. "Yeah, that's what he thinks. He wants to get a job as a private eye."

Several laughed at Cathy's jibe, but Richard turned to the uncomfortable boy. "Let them laugh, Evan. When you make headlines for cracking your first big case, they won't laugh anymore." Evan smiled appreciatively. "Really," Richard continued, "the world needs good detectives. You could be a police inspector, or have a private agency, or be an investigative reporter for a newspaper, or work for the FBI. There's really no limit."

"Well, I guess I'd better see if I can solve this one first. Then maybe I'll apply to Scotland Yard. We were in London last summer, and I loved it there—all those castles and armor . . . and then there's the food," Evan ended appreciatively, taking another helping of the roast lamb with mint sauce.

At first it was hard for Elizabeth to feel involved in the playacting around her. Why concentrate on a pretend mystery when there was a real one upstairs? And yet she knew she must or she would attract unwanted attention. So when a circus was announced as the evening's entertainment, she applauded as excitedly as everyone else.

"A group of traveling performers were stranded when their wagons bogged down in the mud on the moors, and Nigel Cass has graciously consented to let them spend the night in the servants' quarters at Kilcliffe Manor. Provided, of course, that they perform for us in return," Weldon Stark explained.

"Isn't it great the way they do everything in character!" Irene applauded, then groaned and pushed her half-eaten dish of cream and custard trifle away. "But I won't be doing anything but fat-lady characters if I keep this up."

"Oh, Irene—" An idea had suddenly occurred to Elizabeth. "You follow theatre world happenings. Have you heard anything of Margo Lovell recently?"

Irene scrunched her face in thought. "Margo Lovell? English actress? Oh, yes, I remember what marvelous reviews she got for the revival of 'The Duchess of Malfi'."

"What actress was that?" Benton asked.

"Margo Lovell. Elizabeth asked if I knew what'd become of her. I don't think I've heard of her since she played the Duchess of Malfi."

"She died, didn't she? Heart attack or something sudden a few years ago?"

Before Elizabeth could comment on the unfairness of one so beautiful and talented dying young, everyone started moving toward the parlor, and Gavin requested the honor of escorting Elizabeth.

"I haven't been to a circus since I was six years old," Elizabeth said with a laugh. As she took Gavin's arm, she thought that the timing of the event couldn't have been more perfect. If ever there was a time that she needed to escape into the magical fantasy of a circus, it was now. Now, when the real world held a cooling, stiffening, dead body in the room upstairs.

Nothing could have been farther removed from a funeral atmosphere than the parlor. It had been turned into a big top with flying flags, calliope music, and curtains of red velvet and purple satin across one end of the room. Risers provided seating along both walls. Gavin held Elizabeth's hand to help her to an empty spot about halfway up, then settled himself beside her.

Elizabeth was torn between watching the cavorting clowns mingling with the crowd or concentrating on the audience itself, which presented a fashion show of sleek, bias-cut satin dresses, white furs, and diamond jewelry.

"Oh, look at the Navy uniform!" Elizabeth pointed Gavin's attention to a tall man with military bearing just entering the room. "I wonder if he's really Navy or if that's a costume?"

"I think it's a costume. I noticed him earlier. He's sporting some rather irregular-looking badges and medals."

"Oh, good. He's coming our way, maybe we can ask him," Elizabeth said hopefully.

To Elizabeth's delight, the captain and his wife, who was adorned in a dove gray satin gown with a train, sat right in front of her and Gavin. "We've been admiring your uniform," Elizabeth said, as the officer removed his white dress cap and ran his hand across his shiny black hair. He turned at Elizabeth's words, and she saw his shoulder patch—a yellow and orange sunburst with the word *Arizona* across it. "Oh, you're from the *Arizona?*"

"Yes, that's right. I'm on leave from the USS *Arizona*. We've just completed a cruise to the West Indies with President Hoover aboard."

"How nice you could get leave to come to Kilcliffe," Gavin commented, once again in character, twirling his eyepiece on its black ribbon.

"Yes, we've been stationed in the Pacific since '21, so trips to England are a rarity. But I'll retire in '42, which is only nine more years. My wife and I plan to travel a lot then."

It was just playacting, but Elizabeth couldn't stop the chill that spread over her, knowing that just such situations and conversations undoubtedly had occurred in real life. "You're stationed in Pearl Harbor?" She couldn't keep the tremor out of her voice.

"That's right," the man said, beaming. "Beautiful there—palm trees, blue seas and skies—couldn't ask for a better home port."

"Er . . . do you think you might be able to get leave in December of '41?"

"You know," the captain sounded dumbfounded, "you must be the twentieth person to say something like that. 'Stay off boats on Sundays,' everyone says. Makes me wonder what they know that I don't. You don't suppose this whole crowd is psychic, do you?"

"Well, our team *is* Blithe Spirit, but none of us claim to be the seer that Madam Arcati was." Elizabeth gave a light answer, but her laughter was forced.

Her discomfort was soon forgotten though, as all attention shifted to the ringmaster, spotlighted in the center of the room. "Ladies and gentlemen, we are most happy to be with you tonight and to welcome you to the 1933 edition of the Friendly Brothers' Circus!" he proclaimed in southern European dialect.

The acts were introduced at a breathless pace as jugglers, clowns, acrobats, trained animals, and tumblers spun, balanced, and dived around the ring, all of which produced enthusiastic cheers from the audience. To the captivating strains of "Bolero," a sequin-clad trapeze artist entwined her limbs and swirled around a rope hanging from the high ceiling. Sensuous as a snake, the glittering beauty held everyone breathless as her body straightened out in a sharp right angle from the vertical rope and then, with ever-increasing intensity, twirled and spun in response to the mesmerizing music.

When the act was over, Elizabeth caught her breath and clapped until her hands stung. "Bravo! Good show!" her companion shouted. And then they quieted, as the ringmaster directed their attention to "The Magic of Gulamerian." In a sleight-of-hand performance, as fast-paced as the rest of the show, objects appeared, disappeared, and reappeared at Gulamerian's command: Silk scarves fluttered, birds took wing, and balls twirled and bounced.

At the magician's request, a man from the audience donated a paper bill—a one hundred dollar bill—which Gulamerian marked, then 'accidentally' burned. In an effort to direct attention from his blunder he turned quickly to the next act: An egg, a lemon, and an orange, which changed places with one another under silver cylinders in perfect choreography. Suddenly, only the orange could be found. So the orange was peeled to reveal the lemon inside; the lemon sliced to produce the egg; and the egg broken to produce the marked one hundred dollar bill, only slightly soggy with egg yolk.

The audience applauded, and lightheartedness bounced on the air, as unburdened as the pins, balls, and rings kept aloft by Lottie Brunn, "Europe's fastest woman juggler." Her fleet motions of arms and legs kept countless objects aloft to the breathless rhythms of "The Ritual Firedance."

Then, as the acts spun before Elizabeth's giddy senses in a joyous grand finale, the room suddenly came alive with dancing balloons, bounding on their strings as lightly as the bubbles of merriment that had filled the performance. Gavin caught at the string of a bright red, dancing balloon and presented it to Elizabeth with a light kiss on her cheek, which made her heart leap and bob like the balloons.

As if propelled by their balloons, Elizabeth and Gavin followed the clowns leading the procession down the stairway and along the corridor to the West Room Cantina. There a small orchestra played, and a midnight buffet of fruit and cheese snacks offered endless nibbling. Gavin ushered her to a red and white gingham-covered table in a softly lit corner and promised to return in a moment with food and drink. With dream-filled, half-closed eyes Elizabeth watched a few couples dancing on the small center floor and the balloons dancing on the ends of their strings.

When Gavin returned with their drinks and a plate piled high with tasty tidbits, Elizabeth smiled lazily. "Happy?" he asked.

"Delirious!" She took a sip of cherry-red punch, "It's such a . . . a party atmosphere, I can almost believe it is 1933." She had almost said it was a romantic atmosphere, but didn't want to sound pushy. Then Richard walked by, his arm held tightly by a smiling Anita. Even in her three-inch, diamanté heels, her little velvet hat with the eye veil barely reached Richard's shoulder. Elizabeth waved, then turned to Gavin. "Aren't they darling together? I do hope something comes of that. He has been so lonesome ever since his wife died."

Gavin studied her for a moment. "You're sincere, aren't you. I thought perhaps you and he . . . "

"Oh, no. Not at all. I'm sure it must look that way, but we're really just colleagues—and friends, of course. That's why I want him to find someone. I know how lonely he is."

Gavin nodded. "I think I can understand a bit."

Elizabeth remembered the conversation at

dinner about the sudden death of the actress with whom he had been pictured. Yes, Sir Gavin Kendall had known bereavement, too. That caused an ache that no amount of success, money, or titles could soften. She laid her hand on his arm, and he covered her hand with his own. They sat there for some time, listening to the music, watching the festivities around them. Occasionally Gavin gave her hand a small squeeze. Sometimes they nibbled at their refreshments. Now and then one of them would make a comment . . . but mostly, they were just happy together.

At the end of a long, dreamy, orchestral number, they unclasped their hands to applaud the band and dancers, then Elizabeth gave a deep sigh. "It's all such a fantasy, like walking through the screen into a movie set . . . " She frowned thoughtfully.

"I have the feeling you're about to turn philosophical on me," Gavin said.

"You don't mind, do you? Fruit punch has that effect on me." She took a drink, emptying her glass, then shook her head at his offer to refill it for her. "No thanks. Actually, I was thinking that the circus was a perfect metaphor for the thirties. The image was working fine, then I thought maybe the whole thing was symbolic of life and I got rather lost."

"Tell me the part that made sense."

"Well, the circus was such a marvelous escape,

THE CASTLE OF DREAMS

and in the thirties the whole nation had stomachs half-filled by the breadlines, yet people scraped together pennies to attend movies set in posh, all-white, art nouveau apartments and glittering nightclubs. For those few hours, they escaped into another world where they had bigger-than-life glimpses of a happier existence. And that was what made the everyday dreariness bearable."

"Are you saying that's bad or good?"

"I think it's good; dreams are essential. You know, without a vision the people perish. But it can go too far. Do you suppose such escapism was partly responsible for the head-in-the-sand attitudes that made people fail to listen to Churchill and others? Those who warned all through the thirties that Hitler must be stopped before it was too late?" Elizabeth shuddered at the cost of such lack of vision.

"You think too much." Gavin took her hand and pulled her to her feet, then into his arms, as their feet found the rhythm of the foxtrot that the orchestra was playing. Elizabeth lost all sense of time—and certainly all desire to be philosophical—as she and Gavin moved around the room together.

It could have been hours later when the orchestra played the last dance, and the few dancers left on the floor applauded wearily, then turned toward their rooms.

"Shall we go up now?" Gavin looked at his watch.

Elizabeth nodded, and soon they were walking slowly, arm in arm, down a long, deserted corridor. The only sound was the swishing of Elizabeth's ankle-length silk skirt. Their red and yellow balloons followed behind them, tugging lightly at their strings. Gavin paused before a secluded alcove with a tiny velvet loveseat set beside a wicker screen. "Its frightfully late, but . . . "

Elizabeth smiled. There was no need for him to finish his sentence—she had been hoping for a moment alone with him. As they sat on the small sofa she realized this was the first time they'd been alone together since he kissed her in the gazebo. Was that really only yesterday? So much had happened since then.

As he kissed her now, all her earlier thoughts of fantasy and reality, of dreams and actuality, blended in the real-life, dream-come-true experience that Gavin Kendall brought to her.

This fantasy wasn't heedless escapism or an evasion of reality. It was truer than anything Elizabeth had ever experienced, and she was more truly alive, more completely herself, than she had ever felt before.

7

Thursday

A short time later, Elizabeth drifted off to sleep to dream of living in a castle in the air with Gavin. But then her dream twisted and slid, and every bathtub and bed in her castle had a body in it—all the same body, an older man with graying sandy hair matted on his forehead and a narrow mustache that looked like a dark gash against his bloodless skin. Then all the corpses opened their eyes and stared at her, and she screamed and backed away. . . .

"Elizabeth, Elizabeth!" Richard's voice penetrated her screams, and she sat up with a start.

Richard was at her door, pounding on it and calling to her. Shakily, she drew on her robe and went to let him in.

"Are you all right?" he asked, his face etched with concern.

"Oh, I was dreaming . . . it was so awful! They all stared at me, and then they sat up, and

I thought they were coming after me—," she broke off, covering her face with her hands.

Richard put a comforting arm about her and held her tightly. "Who was coming after you?"

"The bodies . . . that man next door. There were lots of him—and—"

"Shhh, easy now, it was just a dream." He stroked her back, as if quieting a high-spirited horse.

Slowly her trembling stopped, and Richard moved to turn on a light. Elizabeth took a deep breath and was sufficiently returned to normal to want to comb her hair. "You know," she said, turning from her mirror after a few flicks of her comb, "I didn't really look at the body yesterday. I think that was a mistake. Do you still have the key?"

Richard frowned. "You mean you want to go back in there?"

"Yes, I do." Elizabeth's voice held unshakable determination. "I need to lay the ghost to rest. No reality will be as bad as the leering images in my head."

Richard nodded and turned to the door. "OK, give me three minutes."

He returned quickly, wearing jeans and a sweater and carrying the key. "You're sure about this?"

She nodded. "I'm sure."

The key turned easily in the door, and Richard clicked on the ceiling light before stepping aside to let Elizabeth in. She walked to the bed, turned back the covers with a steady hand, and looked at the still form there. She took a deep breath. "I knew it wouldn't be so bad. His eyes are rather sunken and his lips dry, but he looks better than they sometimes do at a funeral—more natural."

Richard was close beside her. "Maybe there was some sense to the old-fashioned idea of making children touch a member of the family who died so that they wouldn't miss them so much later."

"Could be. How old do you think he was? Late fifties?"

"I'd guess maybe a bit older—early sixties. He wasn't too big, but he looks like he was in good condition. But then, even olympic athletes have heart attacks," Richard said.

"I hope they can find out something about him. He must have a family somewhere, or something. I know it's silly to judge by appearances, but he doesn't look like a criminal."

She stood in silence for a moment.

"Are you ready?" Richard touched her shoulder.

"Just a minute—like you were saying about that Victorian tradition . . . " She reached out and touched the man's hand that the doctor had laid on his chest. It felt surprisingly soft and pliable; cool, but not cold. Nothing horrible about it, but nothing at all like a human hand, either. She withdrew her hand, then jumped back with a gasp as the arm slid to the bed.

Richard's arm was around her. "Don't worry, you just bumped the mattress."

She laughed weakly. "Of course, I didn't realize I was so skittish. Maybe I should take up going to scary movies or something to get hardened."

Richard covered the body again, turned out the light, and locked the door behind them. "Do you think you can sleep now? It's still an hour or two till daybreak."

"Not a chance. I'm going to get dressed and brew some coffee with that instant water heater thing in the room. Want some, too?"

"Sure. Might as well light the fire in the parlor to keep us company while we're at it."

In a couple of minutes, Elizabeth, dressed in jeans and a sweatshirt, set two mugs on the table in front of the hearth. "Well, the water didn't really boil and the instant powder is kind of weak, but if you tell yourself it's coffee, your tastebuds might believe it."

They sipped their drinks in silence until Elizabeth looked over at the book Richard had brought in to read. "Richard! *The Body Stiffens!* That's not Dante—you're reading a mystery!"

He grinned at her. "When did I ever refuse to do anything you asked me to?"

"The last time I asked you to teach an extra class, as I remember."

"Unfair. You know the academic council sets schedules."

"Seemed worth a try," she said, laughing. "Well, what do you think of it?" She indicated the book. "Got it figured out yet?"

"I'm only on the second chapter. All this time they thought the headmistress was just asleep. Now the maid found her, stiff as a board. You've read it?"

When Elizabeth didn't reply he looked at her. "You've read this one?" he repeated.

Elizabeth still didn't answer, but just sat staring into the fire. Richard frowned in concern. "Elizabeth! Taking you in there wasn't a good idea. I was afraid—"

"No, I'm fine." She gave herself a little shake and looked at Richard. "There's just something wrong. Something bumping and tickling in the back of my brain that I can't get ahold of . . . you know, like when you can't think of the name of a song and it drives you half crazy."

"Try thinking of something else, and it'll probably come to you."

"Good idea." She reached over to an end table where she had set her book of short stories, and they read in companionable silence until it was time to get ready for the day.

Today Elizabeth chose the jaunty middy outfit she had rented—the cheery white tam with a red pompom on the top was just what she needed after that night, and the navy pleated skirt and low-waisted white sailor top had a fresh crispness that Elizabeth's mirror told her she lacked. *Maybe I can work in a nap this afternoon,* she offered herself as consolation.

After breakfast everyone went to the parlor, now returned to its usual sedate condition with rows of chairs, showing no signs of its service as a circus tent the night before. Millie's promised interview was raising a lot of speculation among the sleuths. Evan, sitting next to Elizabeth, took out his notebook and ran over the list of questions he wanted to have answered.

Elizabeth had been so caught up in the events of the past day that she had practically forgotten about the game they had all come there to play. "That's a good idea, Evan," she said, noticing the boy's action. "I should make some notes of my own. I'm afraid I haven't been really concentrating on this puzzle."

Evan looked at her wide-eyed. "How come? You'd better get with it. We won't win if we don't all work at it."

"I'm afraid you're right. I'll try to do better." Elizabeth looked back over her notes from Tuesday's interviews and began drawing arrows at the statements that needed following up.

Her work was interrupted by Weldon Stark. "Our Millie has had a rather trying time, but she's recovered enough now to tell us about it. Millie, what happened?"

"Well, Guv'nor, I don't rightly know. I was

peelin' the potatoes for dinner when I 'ears a noise behind me. I turned around just as 'e grabbed me. I struggled a bit, then I was 'it over the 'ead. Next thing I knows, I was under a table all trussed like a goose with my 'ead 'urting something awful." She rubbed her head behind the little white lace cap.

Stark took the microphone again. "Millie, I'm sure you want to thank the members of the Circle team who rescued you."

Millie's words of thanks were drowned in the cheers from the team contemplating its bonus points.

"And now," Stark continued, "our detective friends here are just itching to ask you some questions, Millie. You give them the best answers you can, my girl."

"Yes, Guv'nor." Millie curtsied as Stark took his seat, then she pointed to a raised hand on the front row.

Elizabeth, sitting in the middle of the room couldn't hear the question, but Millie's answer was clear. "No, sir. I didn't see 'im what attacked me."

"Him?" The audience responded as one person, registering the use of the masculine pronoun.

"That is to say, I didn't see no one— 'im or 'er," Millie amended.

"Do you have any idea why someone would want to do away with you?"

"Did you poison the soup?"

"Do you know who the murderer is?"

The questions tumbled out on top of each other, but Millie's answers were all negative. Evan's politely raised hand received no attention, so this time he jumped to his feet. "Have you remembered anything more about that argument you heard between Gloria and Nigel?"

"Well, yes, sir, you might say as wot I 'ave. Miss Gloria was accusing Mr. Nigel of stealing from 'er. She said she 'ad suspected it for a long time because as 'ow she never 'ad enough ready money, but now she 'ad proof."

Nigel, sitting in the second row, jumped to his feet. "That's a lie! As likely as not you were stealing from her, and you're trying to put the blame on me!" He started forward, shaking his fist at Millie. "You said at first that you didn't hear what was said, and now you come up with this cocklolly story! Well, it won't work! You can't put the blame on me!"

He started forward again, and Stark restrained him. "Maybe you would like to tell us what was said then?" he asked Nigel.

"I certainly would! Gloria was unhappy because I signed her to a run-of-the-mill play contract for her new show, and she wanted out to go on a honeymoon. It was as simple as that. Everyone knows Gloria was loaded. She was a very rich woman precisely because I did such a good job managing her business affairs. It's a sure thing she wouldn't have had two nickles to rub together if I hadn't—that dame didn't have any more business sense than an orangutan."

"All right, Mr. Know-It-All," Millie challenged, "if Miss Gloria 'ad so much money, 'ow is it that she couldn't pay my wages?"

Nigel couldn't seem to think of an answer for this, so Millie, quick to see when she had the upper hand, went on. "Three months behind, she woz. But she said she 'ad expectations, and if I'd just be patient, I'd soon get a nice raise. Well, I said I'd been patient, but a girl 'as to live. But she said as 'ow she'd make it worth my while. So I stayed on."

A questioner from the back called out, "Did she give any indication what these expectations were?"

Millie shook her head, then shrugged. "She said as 'ow she 'ad an insurance policy buried in the family vault."

"And what did you make of that?"

"I didn't make nothin'. Just what she said— she must 'ave some inooity or somethin' in the bank."

"Is 'buried in the family vault' an English expression for 'in the bank'?" a player called out.

"No, Guv'nor, I took it to mean more like safe as 'ouses, as you might say."

"Well, 'safe as houses' isn't something I might say, but I take your meaning. Thank you,

Millie." Stark relaxed his grip on the now-quiet Nigel.

Elizabeth glanced over her notes as the questioning went on. Most of the information she wanted had been covered, but one area seemed to have been overlooked by everyone. She hesitated before raising her hand—if it was important, she would be giving the clue to all the teams, but there was really no other way to follow up on her idea because Stark's rules forbade collaring a suspect and questioning them privately. She raised her hand, then waved it when she was overlooked. "Yes, Mum?" Millie pointed to her.

"Your sister told you she could write a better story than Linden Leigh. Do you know if she ever actually wrote one?"

"Oh, yes, Mum. And it were ever so good, too."

"Do you mean you read it?" Elizabeth tried to find her notes on Millie's first interview. She thought she remembered Millie saying she never read anything.

"Well, no, Mum. Not exactly read it." Millie shifted uneasily from one foot to the other. "But I saw it, I did."

Elizabeth was curious that Millie suddenly seemed so embarrassed. "You saw the manuscript? But you didn't read it? Is that correct? Will you please explain that to us?"

"Well," Millie twisted her hands together. "I

don't mean no disrespect to my sister, 'er bein'
dead and all, but I don't care much for reading.
I mean, when I get a chance to sit down, a nice
spot of the wireless is whot I enjoy. But Vicky
did give me a copy to read—in her own
'andwritin'—and I valued it, I really did. And
I'm not a careless person. I been well trained to
look after Miss Gloria's jools and all, and I
never 'ad no complaints against me, but, well, I
lost it . . . " She finished with her head down.

"You lost your sister's original manuscript?
She must have been terribly upset!" Elizabeth
and Millie were uninterrupted in their dialogue,
while all the players took notes.

"No, Mum. By then she were in 'ospital . . . "
Millie took a moment to compose herself. "I
wouldn't want you to think I was arguin' with
the Almighty, but it do seem unfair, 'er bein'
the one with all the education and all, to die so
young."

"Your sister was well educated?"

"Yes, Mum, me 'af sister, to be exact. She
always did take to books. So our uncle 'elped
'er a bit, and she took night classes and all.
Seemed a terrible drudge for a pretty young
thing, but she loved it. Never got to put it to
no use, though."

"What were you hit over the head with?"

"Were you dragged or carried to where you
were hidden?"

"What kind of knots were you tied with?"

The questions changed focus, and Millie replied that she didn't know what she was hit with; she was probably carried because there "weren't no ladders" in her stockings; and she didn't know anything about knots, but they looked like a kind that might be used to tie up a boat with.

"Mr. Cass, were you ever in the Royal Navy?"

"Do you own a sailboat?"

The private eyes all turned to Nigel's seat, but he had fled from the room.

"Mr. Stark," a questioner called from the balcony at the rear, "are we going to get a chance to view the stiff?"

Elizabeth gasped and grabbed Richard's arm with both hands. "I just remembered the name of the song."

"What are you talking about?"

"The thing that was bothering me—like a tune you can't remember the name of—I know now. Let's go to the room."

"We're having a team meeting now, and then lunch—" Richard hesitated.

"Make some excuse. Ask Bill Johnson to take charge. Say I'm sick." She rushed from the room.

Richard caught up with her a minute later on the stairs. "What is it?"

"I don't want to talk here." They hurried on to the room.

"Now, tell me." Richard pushed the door shut behind him.

"Stiff. That man referred to Gloria as a stiff. She would be by now. And the man next door should be—but he isn't."

"How do you know?"

"The Body Stiffens. The whole thing turned on time of death, and it was established by when rigor mortis set in and went off and all that. I can't remember the times exactly, but I know that body should have been stiff by last night if he died when they said. Something's wrong."

8

Elizabeth looked at Richard wide-eyed, trying to absorb the importance of her own words. "You'd better go get the doctor."

Richard snorted. "That guy barely knew enough to declare the man dead."

"Well, we need more information. You haven't come to that part in the novel yet, have you?"

Richard shook his head. "We need something more solid than a novel, no matter how gripping it may be."

"Well, there's a lot of detective handbooks and criminology texts and things like that in the library."

"There are?"

"I noticed them the other day. I figured they probably use them for these mystery weeks sometimes."

"Yes, I suppose that's likely." Richard turned

to the door. "Everyone will be at lunch now; this is probably a good time to have a look."

A few minutes later, Elizabeth ran her finger down the row of old books. "These must have been purchased secondhand. They look pretty out of date."

Richard smiled grimly. "Well, some things like the facts of death don't really change."

Elizabeth pulled out a book and sank into a chair, turning the pages in concentration. "Here it is . . . 'rigor mortis, temporary stiffening of muscles after death . . . ' they get awfully technical, but it looks like it generally begins to set in within two or three hours, in the jaw and fingers first . . . it lasts twelve to eighteen hours . . . and goes off twenty-four to thirty-six hours after the time of death."

Richard took the book from her hands and scanned the page. "Then that would mean that if Dr. Pearsall was right about our friend dying at one o'clock yesterday . . . "

Elizabeth nodded. "That's what I said. By the middle of the night he should have been stiff. But he wasn't—he was soft when I touched him, and then I bumped the bed, and his arm fell limp. Richard . . . this scares me." She put her hand to her throat.

"No, wait a minute—there's probably a logical explanation. Of course, the doctor said he was guessing . . . maybe the man had just died."

"No, Dr. Pearsall said he was cool. That

would take some time, surely—I don't know. . . .
Do you think the doctor's on the level? But even
if he didn't die until just before we found him,
which was about three o'clock, he still should
have been pretty rigid by the middle of the
night."

"Well, it was rather warm in the room, the
book said that would make a difference." But
Richard didn't sound very convinced.

Elizabeth, however, was happy to grasp at any
logical straw. "Yes, that's true. Let's read some
more and see what we can learn—maybe something more specific on body temperature."

Richard began on the criminology texts, leaving the coroner's handbook to Elizabeth. Richard made a few notes as he went, but Elizabeth
read several pages without finding anything interesting. Then, "Oh, here it is. 'The body loses
one and a half degrees the first hour, one degree
the second, and half a degree every hour after
that to the temperature of its environment.'
Well, I don't know that that's too helpful." She
made a face and read on in silence.

The clock on the mantle chimed the half hour
before either of them spoke, then Richard broke
the silence, "There's some interesting stuff here.
Do you know anything about lividity?"

"What?"

"It has to do with the settling of the blood."
He looked on a bit farther, then read some of it
aloud, "' . . . settles to the lowest parts of the

body . . . begins to show up four hours after death—fully established in six to eight hours . . . '" He turned the page. "Mmmm, where blood settles skin will look bruised, but pressure points will be white . . . Once established, lividity can't be changed by moving the body position or by massage or anything like that . . . "

"Richard," Elizabeth's voice was small and tight. "I think we'd better take another look at that body."

"Oh, there you two are. We missed you at lunch."

"Richard, I haven't seen you all day."

"Bill said you weren't feeling well, Elizabeth."

Blithe Spirit airily invaded the library, with Anita making a beeline for Richard. Elizabeth noted with satisfaction that although Anita's fringed sleeveless dress was perhaps more 1920s than 1930s, it suited her perfectly, and Richard didn't appear unappreciative.

"Well, guess what you missed?" Irene held the center of the stage.

"What?" Elizabeth took the bait, knowing Irene would tell her anyway and not at all unhappy to have something lighter to think about.

"Susie confessed."

"Confessed? Susie? I don't believe she had the gumption to commit a murder," Elizabeth said.

"What did she say?" Richard asked.

"Well, we were just all eating lunch, and they served this wonderful fruit pudding for dessert, when there was some kind of a row at the table where the actors were sitting. All of a sudden, Susie jumped up and ran to the center of the room." Irene suited her actions to her narrative. "'All right! I can't take any more! I confess—I did it! I'd been jealous of her for years, and seeing her become Lady Leigh was just more than I could take, so I put poison in her water.' Then she broke down sobbing, and Stark led her off."

"Well, does anyone believe it?" For the first time, the lawyer took charge.

"I don't know, she sounded sincere," Cathy said.

"Yeah, but then she's an actress," Cathy's brother argued with her.

"Her motive seems weak compared to some of the others."

The discussion became general as questions and theories came from every side of the library.

"Maybe she lied about not loving Sir Linden."

"But what motive could she have for confessing if she didn't do it?"

"Where would she get poison?"

"What would work that fast?"

"Cyanide."

"Aha! Spies carry cyanide. She was Brian Rielly's girlfriend."

"Did she commit the murder for Brian?"

"Or confess to protect her lover?"

"That newspaper article said there was a security leak. I'm sure that was secrets Brian told Gloria when they were going together."

"But it seems clear that Nigel abducted Millie—that doesn't fit in at all."

"But what does fit is that if Gloria was desperate for money because Nigel was embezzling, she might have sold state secrets."

"If she was that kind of person, would Sir Linden marry her?"

"Maybe she was blackmailing him."

"All right now, you're speculating. We've got to stick to the facts." Benton brought them back to the evidence.

But Elizabeth couldn't concentrate on the game any longer. There was a job that needed doing upstairs. She caught Richard's eye, and they slipped quietly out the door.

Elizabeth could now look at the body without hesitation, and she even managed a mild joke. "He hasn't moved since we left him."

"Aren't you glad." Richard's smile showed his relief at her new level of comfort.

But inside the room Elizabeth held her nose. "Yuck!"

Richard nodded. "I noticed it, too. I'll open the windows."

Elizabeth lifted the corpse's arm by the coat sleeve and shook it—absolutely no sign of rigidity. "If this is a textbook case, this man was probably already dead for a full day to a day and a half before we found him."

"Right. Died noon Monday at the latest. Well, let's get to it—can't check lividity with all these clothes on." Richard tugged off the man's jacket, then handed it to Elizabeth.

"Hmm, English tweed. Whatever he did, he must have been reasonably successful at it."

Richard dropped the ecru linen shirt on the floor and rolled the body over to examine his back.

"Ooo!" Elizabeth held her hand over her mouth and rushed to the fresh air of the window. After a few gulps she turned back and saw that Richard, too, had moved to uncontaminated air and was still looking a little green. "Are you OK?" she asked with a weak smile.

"Yeah, let's get back to it."

Richard moved with reluctance. "Now if I understand this business right, a man who died in bed would have a purplish-looking back with white patches where the tips of his shoulder blades rested on the bed."

The man's back was colorless.

"How delicate are your sensibilities?" Richard reached around to loosen the man's slacks, then began tugging at them.

"I'm OK. This is purely academic. Besides, I have a brother, you know."

Richard pulled the man's slacks off, and they both looked at the sight, speechless.

"Well, that tells the story."

Elizabeth gulped. "I think this is where some-one should say, 'Not a very pretty sight, is it?'"

On the man's backside, from thighs to waist, even showing through the open-weave knit of his shorts, the skin was a deep purplish black, as if all the blood in his body had drained there—as indeed, it had. And oddly, there was a white leaf-shaped mark high on one thigh and a sim-ilar design on the opposite leg.

"Well, let's finish this while we're at it," Eliza-beth said. She leaned over and pulled a sock off the white foot. "Richard, this man did not hike in over any back trail through the mud and rain—his socks are spotless."

"The more we learn the less I like it. All of a sudden nothing fits." Richard reached for the last piece of clothing. "Interesting underwear, I've never seen anything like it."

"I have," Elizabeth said.

Richard was so surprised he dropped the waistband around the man's knees and gaped at Elizabeth. "What?"

"I told you I wasn't squeamish about men's underwear. I always used to buy them for my brother. That kind—exactly that kind. They were only available one place in the US, from a supplier that sells British army surplus." Then she added with an air of exaggerated supe-riority, "I told you my catalog reading was use-ful."

"What's so useful about knowing where a corpse ordered his underwear?"

"Because I always ordered Taylor's shorts for him, until three years ago when Brit-Wear quit carrying them. See the label on those? Unfaded. New. My dear Watson, this man is from England, possibly military."

"Maybe." Richard turned back to the body. "But what do you make of that?"

The man's right hip bore the white imprint of a five-petaled flower, a shape as distinct as a brand on a horse. Elizabeth stared for a moment. "White means pressure point. Is there a design on the mattress? Or did he have something that shape in his hip pocket?"

Richard pulled up the sheet to examine the mattress, and Elizabeth reached for the trousers at the foot of the bed.

"These slacks don't have back pockets."

"There's no design on the mattress, but look." Richard pointed to a reddish brown stain on the sheet by the man's mouth. "I wonder what that means?"

"We could probably find out from some of those books . . . but I'm not sure I want to."

They looked at each other for a moment. "Well, can we do anything else here?"

Elizabeth shook her head, "I don't think so; just cover him up." She walked to the open window, gulping fresh air and gazing out on the rocky terrain. It hadn't rained much for two days now; surely the crews would have that road open soon. Then the management could call the police. From what she and Richard had seen, it was clear that the body had been moved to this bedroom *after* the man was dead. And that could only mean one thing: there was a killer in the hotel.

9

Back in her sitting room, Elizabeth sat limply in one of the wing-backed chairs by the fireplace. "But it's so awful. How could anyone do that to another human being? I mean, it's OK as a game . . . Gloria Glitz was just acting, and it gives us all an interesting intellectual puzzle to work on. But in real life—to take a life that God created—I'm surprised God doesn't strike murderers down on the spot with thunderbolts."

Richard nodded, but didn't interrupt her monologue.

"After seeing that poor man, I can't understand some people's soul-searching over bringing a criminal to justice. I have the most unholy reaction of wanting to see whoever did that nailed to the wall. In one of the Wimsey mysteries Lord Peter spent the night one murderer was being executed grieving in his wife's arms. I'm afraid I would have been celebrating "

"No, you wouldn't," Richard said quietly. "Human life is human life—all created by God and holy in his sight. The recognition of that fact is a tremendous thing. Probably only Jews and Christians can truly appreciate the sanctity of human life. It was all created by God for a purpose, no matter how far that person may have strayed from the divine image."

Elizabeth sat up straighter in her chair—if anything could bring her out of a depression it was discussing God and her favorite literary genre. "Yes! That's what I taught my students in that whodunit class you disapproved of—that ultimately mysteries are one of the most moral forms of fiction because they bring order out of chaos and punish evil. The good ones do, anyway. I think the new vogue for letting the criminal win is one of the worst forms of obscenity. . . " Her voice trailed away as she remembered Gavin's praise for just such books. She sat back in her chair.

A knock at the door made her sit up again. Richard opened it to Gavin, and Elizabeth gasped. "Oh, I'm so sorry, Gavin, I lost all track of time. Is it really dinner time already?"

"Almost. I came a bit early. What had you so engrossed?"

Elizabeth laughed. "My favorite subjects, mystery-writing and theology. Will you wait while I change, Gavin? Richard, aren't you meeting Anita soon?"

Richard groaned. "Oh, I nearly forgot."

Elizabeth heard Gavin say, "You two did get involved, what?" as she closed her door behind her. In a few minutes she reopened it, now clad in a rosy peach, clingy crepe skirt and a satin top with a deep, ruffled neckline and long sleeves. Her head was wrapped in a turban-style band of matching fabric, which was pinned in place with her grandmother's pearl-and-diamond brooch.

Gavin stood at her entry. "I say, that was worth waiting for."

Elizabeth held out her hand to him as she crossed the room. "If you men just realized how stunning you look in formal wear, the tradition of dressing for dinner would return tomorrow."

"Complete with boiled shirts?" He took her hand, bowed over it, and tucked it under his bent elbow.

"I've never been quite sure what that meant when I read it in a book. I assume it meant shirts that were very white and very stiff."

"And very uncomfortable. Something only one to the manner born could wear with comfort," Gavin said.

"The true test, like *The Princess and the Pea.*" Talking nonsense with Gavin was such fun.

But at the Blithe Spirit table the conversation wasn't considered nonsense by its participants:

"You're crazy!" Evan hit the table, making his sister pull back, startled.

"No, I'm not! I'm sure he did it all alone.

Susie didn't know anything about the murder. But she loves him so much she'll protect him, even if it means jail for her."

"In the thirties it wasn't jail, it was the electric chair—remember when we went to Madame Tussaud's in London?"

Cathy shuddered but held her ground. "Well, that's how much she loves him."

"Brian may be a murderer for the sake of national security, but he's not a total creep," Evan's voice rose. "He wouldn't let a woman take the rap. They planned it together from the first."

"You're both crazy, kids," Bill interrupted his children. "Nigel's our man—why else would he try to get rid of Millie?"

"The fact that Nigel only tied Millie up shows he's not a murderer. He just wanted to keep her out of the way so she couldn't tell about the fight and have everyone learn he was an embezzler."

"Well, I wish you'd get this settled," Irene told them all. "I don't care who you decide did it—I just need to know so I can put our skit together. We have to perform the thing Sunday morning, and some of the groups are practicing already. Private Lives got twenty bed sheets from housekeeping after tea today."

"How do you know?"

"Spies." She held an imaginary magnifying glass to her eye.

"Speaking of spies," Elizabeth turned to Gavin and spoke under her breath. "Richard and I did a spot of undercover work this afternoon. We've got a problem upstairs."

"What?" He gave her his concerned attention.

"That man." She pointed up toward the fourth floor. "The doctor was all wet, or covering something up. That man's been dead for ages, since Tuesday morning at least."

"You mean . . . but we saw him late Monday night . . . that means he must have died shortly after he left your room." Gavin looked stricken. "What a ghastly thought—I sent the poor blighter out with a flea in his ear to meet his death. I may have been the last person to see him alive—" He swallowed deeply. "I say, that takes some getting used to."

Elizabeth put her hand on his arm. "Don't torture yourself; you couldn't have known. But I'm afraid it gets worse. He didn't die in that bed. Someone put him there. You know what that means?"

"I'm very much afraid I do. Who have you told?"

"No one yet, unless Richard told Anita. I suppose Mr. Hamlin should know, but I don't see that much can be done until the police can get here. I suppose they could come up in a helicopter if we could get word to them."

"I haven't heard a news report lately, but if the flood conditions have subsided in the valley someone could hike out." Gavin frowned thoughtfully.

Elizabeth was glad he didn't ask for any details about the body—she wanted to enjoy her dinner. And dinner that night was most enjoyable. It featured a dessert buffet in the center of the room, where the salad bar usually stood. Such creations du chef as Vienna nut torte, Black Forest cake, strawberry parfait, blueberry custard, eclairs and Napoleons, and imported cheeses with strawberries, grapes, and pears adorned a three-tiered table. It left all the diners laughing helplessly at their own greediness, even the brother and sister, who could hardly fight with each other while sharing bites of a chocolate whipped cream cherry confection.

Elizabeth pushed her plate away with a groan.

"Is that a signal you've finished?" Gavin asked.

"That Port Salut is the best cheese I've ever tasted in my life, but when I'm too full even to finish my tea, you know I'm full."

Fixing his glass in his eye, always a signal he was going into a characterization, Gavin leaned toward her. "In that case, my dear, how about coming up to my room for a spot of rare manuscript viewing?"

Elizabeth held up her hand as a warning. "Not unless the butler is there to supervise."

"Alas, the inestimable fellow remained in

London. Hard-hearted of him. I'm desolate without his services."

"Just as I supposed. Besides, you already confessed that you don't collect rare books."

"Careless of me. Well, might as well make the best of it then and go to the movie, what?"

Tonight's film was *The Silent Passenger,* a 1935 period piece with Peter Haddon playing Lord Peter Wimsey. But even the most devoted old movie buff had to admit it was only interesting rather than gripping, and the combination of a comfortable chair, a dark room, a full stomach, and last night's interrupted sleep made it more than Elizabeth could do to stay awake.

She battled through the first half, then decided she was being ridiculous to attempt the impossible. "I'm sorry, Gavin, but I'm so sleepy I just can't fight it any longer."

He glanced quickly at the screen, then back to her. "Of course, I'll take you to your room."

"No. You stay here. I know it's important to you to see Haddon's interpretation, and there's no telling when you'll get to see such an obscure film again."

"Are you sure?"

"Perfectly. I'm quite capable of walking to my room."

The old hotel was quiet, and the uneven floorboards creaked under her feet as she climbed the stairs, her hand running lightly up the oak banister. On the fourth floor the hall was softly lighted, and the mellow wainscoting was warm and welcoming. Elizabeth's mind was full of images from the movie and the role-playing of the past days . . . and suddenly she was walking down the hall in a Yorkshire country house in the thirties.

The sensation lasted only a few seconds before reality intervened and shattered the illusion, but for that moment it had been so absolutely real, so totally authentic, that it left Elizabeth shaken and strangely buoyed. It was as if all the books she had read and the movies she had seen about time travel and visiting other dimensions were possible.

Yet the fact that the moment passed so swiftly left her with a sense of loss and a nostalgic ache for things that could never be recaptured: The fading of a dream, a vision of the night—*like a starving man who dreams and thinks that he is eating, but wakes up to find himself empty, or a thirsty man who dreams and thinks that he is drinking, but wakes up to find himself thirsty and dry.* She frowned slightly, wondering where she had recently read these words . . . Oh yes, they were from Isaiah 29—and as she recalled them now, they only seemed to reinforce her feeling of sadness.

She entered her sitting room with a sigh, pulled the turban and brooch from her head, tossed them on the coffee table, and with a drowsy step went into her bedroom. In a few minutes she slipped into bed, thinking of Gavin, of the delight of being with him, and the incredible experience of seemingly finding her favorite fictional heroes in real life; and, like Sebastion in *The Tempest,* she murmured, "If it be thus to dream, still let me sleep."

10

Friday

The next morning, Elizabeth wakened to the sound of rain being driven against her window by a strong wind. If this weather didn't clear up pretty soon she was going to start worrying about getting home. Being cut off from reality and lost in a fantasy for a few days was fine, but if it went on much longer, claustrophobia would set in. Especially since one of those sharing her confinement was . . . well, never mind . . .

She washed her face vigorously to avoid following that line of thought, then sat down for a few minutes with her Bible. She followed her usual practice of reading, currently in Isaiah, until she found a verse to memorize for the day. A short time later she left her room, feeling refreshed.

Seeing a man in the hall, she opened her mouth to greet Richard, then started when she realized it was someone else. "Oh, Bill. You startled me. What are you doing down that empty hall?" Her eyes flicked to the door of the supposedly empty room just beyond them.

"Just taking a morning constitutional. All this rich food and little chance for exercise—it's starting to catch up with me. Ready for a new day of sleuthing?"

"Er, sure." She forced a smile as she fell into step beside him down the stairs. *What was he doing outside that room?* she wondered.

But at the dining room she met Richard, and his first question changed her train of thought.

"Did you have a nice evening?" he asked, as Bill moved on to join his family.

"I sure did, in spite of getting sleepy in the middle of the movie. Gavin Kendall is really a major league nice person." She smiled, then added quickly, "And so is Anita."

"You noticed that, too, did you?"

They were almost to the Blithe Spirit table when Elizabeth remembered she had left her notebook in the room. "You go on, Richard, I'll catch up."

But the notebook wasn't on the coffee table where she was sure she had left it. She checked the books on the end table, the pile of papers on the desk where Richard had apparently been working at odd moments . . . even under the chairs and sofa. She started to look in her room, checking behind the cushions of the sofa. But all she found was the peach crepe headband she had tossed there lethargically last night. And only the headband. She stared at the fabric lying limp in her hand. No pearl and diamond brooch.

She began to search frantically, pulling the cushions off the sofa, crawling around the floor on her hands and knees, even raking through the ashes in the fireplace. It was gone.

Her first thought was to get to Richard. She turned and barely missed banging into the door as it opened toward her, "Oh, Richard, I'm so glad—"

"Sorry to disappoint and all that, but I told Richard I'd pop up and tell you the news." Gavin put his hands on her shoulders to steady her. "Is something wrong?"

"My brooch, Grandmother's pearls—it's gone."

"So they got to you, too, did they?"

"Too?" She sank into the nearest chair.

"I'm afraid there's been rather a rash of jewel-thieving." Elizabeth's hand went to the slim gold chain at her throat. "Stark announced at breakfast that there were several occurrences last night, which were definitely not part of the scenario. He suggested that everyone turn their valuables in to the hotel to keep them in the safe, and two of the bellboys have been dis-patched to hike down the mountain for the police. Although, in this weather . . . " They both glanced anxiously at the rain-battered window.

"Of course, the good part is that the weather makes it harder for the culprit to get away, too. I think the hotel is quite optimistic about recovering the jewelry."

But Elizabeth wasn't really thinking about the jewelry. "Then, that must mean that our corpse was involved in a jewel ring, and the others bumped him off." She began pacing the room, then laughed. "Oh, dear, I'm talking like a character in a cheap thriller."

"I think you're probably right, though. It does look as though he had a mate. The fellow has probably done us a favor. It's a dead cert, I'd say, that when they solve the robbery they'll solve the murder. Of course, that's not generally known yet."

"And they're going ahead with the game?"

"Full speed. It's more important than ever—keep the troops occupied, so to speak. Matter of fact, I'm on the agenda this morning."

"Oh? I haven't checked my schedule. What's happening?"

"Speeches in the main parlor. Stark on detective technique, Matt Cruise—Brian Rielly to you—on spies in fact and fiction, and yours truly on the classic country-house mystery." He bowed. "But you're missing breakfast."

"It seems discovering I've been robbed took

my appetite away. Maybe I could just grab a
piece of toast along the way."

Gavin was holding the door open for her
when she cried, "Oh, now I remember—I left
my notebook by my bed!" She returned with it
in a minute. "At least that's one mystery
solved."

Weldon Stark's speech on the scientific
aspects of detection, from electronic surveil-
lance to forensic toxicology, was fascinating, but
Elizabeth couldn't keep her mind on the lec-
ture. She found that her thoughts and notes
kept drifting to the real mystery in Eyrie House.

"Because of the perfection of modern meth-
ods of detection and estimation of poisons, poisoning, which was the favorite weapon of the
criminal of bygone days, has declined consider-
ably . . . "

*If they could just identify that little man, some-
how it wouldn't seem so awful. It's just the idea of
a nameless grave . . .*

"The archetype of mineral poisons is arsenic,
which since ancient times, was the poisoners'
favorite . . . "

*He must have been here either as one of the
jewel thieves,* Elizabeth thought, *and they killed
him over a disagreement. Or maybe he was a
policeman, or journalist, or an insurance inspector . . . something like that, tracking the thieves.
Either way, last night's robbery means that the
murderer is among us—actively among us . . .*

She shivered and forced her mind back to Weldon Stark.

"Now, that favorite of all spy thrillers, hydrocyanic acid, is a very volatile liquid smelling of bitter almonds, and fifty milligrams of it is sufficient to cause death. Unfortunately, for the addicted readers of international intrigue, metallic cyanide takes an appreciable time to act, and death commonly follows about thirty minutes later . . . "

Cyanide . . . almond smell . . . thirty minutes . . . Elizabeth's pen stilled as her mind wandered. *Whatever the man's reason was for being at the Eyrie House, he should have had some luggage. A thief would have tools, surely. And a detective would, too—they always do on TV. Whatever he was doing, he would need clothes, a toothbrush, a razor . . . if we could just find his things . . .* She had developed almost a possessive feeling about the man—it was her corpse—after all, she'd found it twice.

" . . . Strychnine is fortunately used less and less as a rat poison, but it used to be popular with would-be poisoners. It is a convulsive poison . . . "

Gavin was next on the program, and Elizabeth struggled to follow his classification of mystery writing into classic detections, gothic thrillers, spy intrigues, occult horrors, and police procedurals. "Wilkie Collins is considered the father of the classic whodunits; most of you have probably read *The Moonstone* . . . "

Elizabeth looked at her notes and saw that instead of writing "Collins," her pen had scribbled "luggage." At that, she abandoned all pretense of listening to the speakers and began concentrating on the most likely places to look for her corpse's possessions. Going on the assumption that he did bring some luggage with him, she figured that one of two things had to have happened: Either he put it someplace himself before he met his murderer and it was still there, or the murderer disposed of it later. If the latter had happened, it could be too late to find anything—although the chances seemed good that the luggage might still be somewhere in the hotel, since there had been so little time when it was possible to go outside.

Let's suppose he put his things someplace himself, Elizabeth thought. *The manager was sure the man wasn't a registered guest, assuming Mr. Hamlin was telling the truth, so he didn't have a room of his own to put anything in . . . I suppose he could have hidden it someplace like one of those crawl cubbys in the hall, but that seems unlikely. If he was one of a team, he might have been sharing a room that one of the others booked. In that case, we're in trouble. Only the police could find his things with a search warrant. But suppose he came alone, intending to check in, but found out the hotel was overbooked, or just that his room wasn't ready yet . . . I don't suppose jewel thieves or people tracking them, whichever he was, make their reservations through travel agents . . .*

A round of applause told Elizabeth she had missed all of Gavin's speech. Hoping she didn't look as guilty as she felt, she applauded enthusiastically and prayed he wouldn't ask her any questions about his talk.

Elizabeth hadn't realized that Brian Rielly was being played by the writer of a TV spy series, but when Matt Cruise began talking about the CIA, KGB, MI5, Interpol, Moscow Centre, and the SAS, she could tell he knew his business. But not even foreign intrigue could hold her thoughts.

I wonder if they have a lost and found . . . surely unclaimed luggage would have been noticed by now. Maybe there's some storage room no one has looked in . . . if he put anything in the safe, surely the manager would have recognized him . . .

Suddenly, Elizabeth's thoughts and Brian's speech were interrupted by a large man in a trilby and belted tan raincoat who strode onto the platform and held out an identification card. "Scott of the Yard here. Brian Rielly, I'll have to ask you to come along with me. Certain parties at Number 10 Downing Street would like to ask you some questions."

Brian, his hands behind him, his head down, was led off the stage. In the confusion that followed, Irene was the first to round up the Blithe Spirit team and herd them into the library.

"Well, what do you think? Does this confirm Brian's guilt?"

The question fell like a bone among hungry dogs.

"I don't think it bears on the case."

"Of course it does, it proves he was the security leak."

"But why murder Gloria after the horses have escaped, or the hose has leaked, or whatever the metaphor is?"

"I think Stark has removed Brian from the action."

Irene stuck two fingers in her mouth and whistled for attention. "OK, like I said yesterday, you guys decide—but hurry up so I can get our act together. Now let me tell you what I have in mind and see if it's OK with everybody. How about being a puzzle? Each one of us can be a piece, and when we fit together it'll make a picture of the murderer."

"That's great!"

"How are you going to do that?"

"I love it!"

"Sounds like a lot of work."

"That's a sure winner!"

The conversation went on, discussing the puzzle idea and arguing about Brian's guilt. Elizabeth caught Richard's eye across the room and motioned toward the door. He excused himself from Anita and joined Elizabeth outside the room.

She explained quickly, " . . . and so I think we might be able to find his luggage or something if we dig a bit."

"I'm game. Let's get a bellboy to help us."

There was a young man in a green Eyrie House shirt near the front desk. "Yes, Ma'am, we have a luggage room. Sometimes tours send luggage ahead, or people arrive before their rooms are ready, or they leave a suitcase behind by mistake." He took a key from a drawer behind the desk and led them to a door a short distance down the hall. "What does your friend's suitcase look like?"

"I'm not sure, he's—er, resting upstairs, and we thought we'd just pick it up for him." Elizabeth wasn't sure if the manager had informed his staff of the events. She didn't want to be the one to spill the beans if he hadn't.

The oversized closet held a few cardboard boxes, an abandoned-looking overcoat, a steamer trunk apparently waiting to be shipped when the road was cleared, and a two-tone brown duffle. "I think that's it." Elizabeth pointed, trying to keep her voice calm.

"Oh, Mr. Parkerson?" The bellboy leaned over and picked up the bag. "I didn't realize he hadn't picked this up yet."

"You mean, you put it in here for him?" Richard asked.

"Yes, he got here before noon Sunday, or was it Saturday? Anyway, the rooms weren't ready for check-in yet, and he asked me to stow it for him as he was in a hurry to meet someone. Surprising he'd wait until the end of the week to get it—most people are in a real toot to get their luggage."

"Yes. Well, thank you for taking care of it for him." Richard tipped the bellboy and took the bag.

Sure the bag contained the answers to all their questions, Elizabeth had a terrible time controlling the urge to run to their room. "Can you believe it was that easy? Just walk in and ask for it! Why didn't someone find it sooner?"

Richard closed the sitting room door behind them. "The classic answer: 'Nobody asked.' Do you think it's all right to open this, or should we wait for the police? Maybe we should at least call the manager or something?"

"Richard!" Elizabeth practically exploded. "If you don't open that, I'm going to! We discovered it, that ought to give us some right. Then you can put it in his room afterward if you want to." She pointed next door.

The bag wasn't even locked. "Clean shirts, more of your British military underwear, toothbrush, toothpaste, razor, socks—our Mr. Parkerson was a light traveler and not very imaginative."

"But isn't there any identification?"

"Hold on a minute." Richard unzipped a small pocket inside the bag. "Here we are." He held up a slim, blue-black booklet blazoned with a gold armorial lion and unicorn. "British passport—score one for the catalog readers." He flipped through the pages to the listing of occupation and held it for Elizabeth to see.

"Detective-Inspector Charles Parkerson, Scotland Yard, retired," she read out loud. She paused for a moment. "He must have found out who Gloria's killer was and . . . Oh! What am I saying? But I never did think he was a criminal. Oh, I'm so glad!"

"Glad?"

"Yes, funny, isn't it? I've become rather fond of the little man. Of course, it'd be easier to accept his death if he were a crook, but—," her voice trailed off. She couldn't really explain how she felt about it.

"Well, now, where does this leave us?" Richard sat on the sofa, still holding the passport. "If our other guesses have been right, he was tracking a jewel thief, presumably from England. Wonder who else is here from England besides Sir Gavin?" Suddenly Richard's eyes widened a little. "Elizabeth, you don't suppose . . . ?"

"Richard!" An angry flush rose in her cheeks, "How could you even think such a thing? There are one hundred guests here, about thirty-five staff members, ten actors—why should Gavin be suspect just because he's the most obvious Englishman? Besides, are only Englishmen allowed to steal jewels in England? Evan Johnson said they were there last summer. I'll bet half the people here travel all the time . . . "

Richard sat quietly and let her rave. After she'd been quiet a few moments he said, "So you thought of it, too?"

"Certainly not." She turned and walked into her own room. She was so confused. She sat on the edge of the bed, her head in her hands. She needed to sort things out, to think straight, but the clues swam in her head, facts and red herrings swimming indistinguishably side by side.

"Think!" she told herself sternly. *OK, someone must have come here planning a robbery—a known jewel thief whom Parkerson was trailing. No, the Scotland Yard man was after a security leak. . . . Did the two cases tie together? No, no! The spy bit was part of the play.*

She groaned and started over. *Someone killed Parkerson because he was going to arrest him, or her—maybe not for the robbery . . . maybe that was a diversion. Maybe he was really tracking a killer. Gloria's murderer! But didn't I read somewhere that master thieves aren't usually murderers?* She hit the bed in frustration. She'd done it again; Gloria's murder wasn't real . . . Parkerson's was. And he certainly wasn't murdered for tracking a stage villain.

Try again: *Someone did something illegal in England, probably a robbery. Parkerson followed that person here and was killed. . . . Gloria accused Nigel of stealing from her . . . Ohhhh!*

Elizabeth groaned, then went to the bathroom and splashed her face with cold water. It wasn't working. Avoiding the central issue was driving her crazy. She had to face it: *Was it possible Gavin could be a suspect? Certainly not, he was engaged to Gloria . . .*

Good grief, she was going insane. Wasn't one of the first symptoms not knowing the difference between fantasy and reality? Had she really crossed some line where she didn't know what was real and what was playacting?

She shook her head. No, of course she hadn't. She just needed to talk through everything. She went to the door and called to Richard, but he wasn't there. He'd probably gone down to lunch. She'd have to work through it herself. But it was so much harder alone.

Immediately with that thought came the answer: She wasn't alone. "Oh, God, thank you for being there!" she breathed gratefully.

Not there. Here. Right here with you.

The relief brought tears to her eyes. "Yes, Emmanuel. God with us." She suddenly had a whole new understanding of the presence of God. She picked up the Bible by her bed, and it fell open at her marker in Isaiah 26: "Thou dost keep in peace men of constant mind, in peace because they trust in thee. Trust in the Lord forever; for the Lord himself is an everlasting rock."

Her heart filled with joy and gratitude—and peace. She turned back a few pages to words she had underlined earlier in the week: "The Lord of Hosts has sworn: In very truth, as I planned, so shall it be; as I designed, so shall it fall out . . ." She closed the book and her eyes. *Dear Lord, I know you have the situation in hand. Now help me find your way. Thank you for being here taking every step with me.*

After a while, she opened her eyes, feeling calm. Now, maybe she could think. She took a deep breath and started again.

Could she trust Gavin? The question seemed so ridiculous. She turned it around: Could she suspect him when the evidence was so slim? Could Gavin Kendall, the man she loved, possibly be guilty of anything as horrible as robbery or . . . or . . .

Her mind refused to finish the question. After all, trust was a major part of love. Surely it wasn't possible for her to love someone unworthy of trust.

What she needed to do was find another suspect, but she knew so little about the other guests. She had hardly spoken to anyone but the members of the Blithe Spirit team. That was the way the game was played. Still, she could name at least one suspect: Bill Johnson had been outside Parkerson's room this morning . . . and he had traveled in England. From every appearance the Johnsons were a wealthy family. Bill had said he was in real estate, but that was a broad field. Had it alone produced the money for the fancy vacations to which his family seemed accustomed?

There was always Anita . . . now she was really grasping at straws . . . but was the glamorous Ms. Crocker sticking so close to Richard because she was attracted to his charms, or because she suspected he knew something about the murder? Had Richard been telling her all that had happened? Ridiculous. Anita was much too small to have moved a body.

OK, what about the hotel staff? Why was Mr. Hamlin so insistent on keeping the death a secret? Was it really for the sake of the hotel—or did he have a more personal motive? How about Dr. Pearsall? Was his mistake about the time of death an innocent error because of his inexperience, or . . . maybe Hamlin and Pearsall were in it together. They could cover for each other and split the takings. Hmm, that made sense. Who would have readier access to all the rooms than the manager? And he would know which rooms were occupied by wealthy guests . . .

Elizabeth smiled and took a deep breath. These were much happier thoughts, more on a level with the detached puzzle of trying to solve a mystery novel before the fictional sleuth. After all, that's what a mystery week was all about, wasn't it?

11

By the time Elizabeth was ready to socialize again, lunch was long past. Since that meant she had missed both meals that day, it took a considerable amount of discipline to maintain a lady-like demeanor at the well-spread tea table gracing the autograph party in the Lake Lounge. Three tomato-and-egg finger sandwiches and two slices of nut bread were all she could balance gracefully at the moment, but she promised her stomach a speedy return for refills as soon as those were downed.

Weldon Stark and Gavin Kendall were sitting at tables piled with copies of their books. Matt Cruise, with Scotland Yard keeping custody close at hand, was autographing copies of *TV Guide* over the listing of his program. Many of the guests were circulating mystery week programs or even tea party napkins for the celebrities to sign.

Irene was standing in line for Sir Gavin's autograph when Elizabeth joined her. "If I had thought to bring a *TV Guide,* I would have you sign it by some of the shows you've been in."

Irene laughed. "Good idea. That may be the only way I'll ever get my name listed. Be sure you watch 'Dallas' in two weeks. I've got a part in that. But don't be late. I'm only in the first ten minutes."

"I'll put it on my calendar."

Irene laughed, but Elizabeth assured her she meant it. Then she looked at the papers in Irene's hand. "What are you having autographed?"

Irene held out a copy of a *Time* magazine book review. "I was so mad at myself for forgetting to bring my copy of *Who Doth Murder Sleep?* that I looked this up in the library and asked the office to photocopy it for me. I loved the book, and I had to have something autographed. Oh, that reminds me, when I was looking through those back issues I found a picture of that actress you were asking me about the other day."

"Margo Lovell?" Elizabeth said the name quietly, not wanting Gavin to hear her talking about his dead girlfriend.

"Yes, her uncle was killed a few years ago in an IRA terrorist attack on the minister of something or other. His body lay in state in Westminster

144

Abbey. It was a picture of her grieving by the casket—very touching in a regal sort of way."

"I'd like to see it."

"I think I left the magazine on the top of the stack—one of the top ones, anyway. In the 'People' section."

The line moved forward, and Irene held out her paper to be signed. Gavin smiled, a bit embarrassed at the extravagant review, and said something to Irene, but Elizabeth was ready to revisit the tea table. This time she concentrated on the tiny round butter cookies and little squares of cake to accompany her refilled cup.

The line waiting to see Gavin was even longer than before, so Elizabeth merely caught his eye and waved to him before moving on around the room. She looked for some of the other Blithe Spirit members; she wanted a chance to question Bill Johnson about his business and travels. She spotted Richard and Anita in a corner by the fireplace, but they didn't look as if they would particularly welcome her intrusion, so she started to take a seat by herself. As she did so, Helen Johnson came up.

"Why don't you go around with us? This is the last chance to interview witnesses, and Evan and Cathy still have several burning questions. I hope to goodness they can resolve this thing—they kept us awake half the night arguing over who did it. I keep telling them it's just a game, but they're really taking it seriously."

Several interviewers were gathered around Millie, who was working herself into an emotional state over the questions being put to her. "I can't see whot that 'as to do with anything. Unless yer think Vicky's ghost came back to murder me for my carelessness and got me mistress instead."

"No, no, Millie. We're sorry we've upset you," a woman in a purple lace afternoon tea gown said soothingly. "But my dear, you must see that we simply have to follow every little lead. Now will you please try to think just once more? Are you absolutely certain you haven't the tiniest inkling where you might have lost your sister's manuscript? Did you take it in a taxi or on a bus? Could you have put it in the back of some closet and it's still there? Do try to think, dear."

Millie shook her head. "No, I never 'ad it in no taxi or omnibus. Vicky gave it to me one night at the theatre and . . . and I don't know. That's all I remember. I were real rushed, and I didn't think of it again for a few days. Then when I did . . . " The witness broke down again.

The soft approach having failed, another player tried something different. "Now see here, young woman. That's quite enough of this sniveling. I believe you're doing it to hide something. Maybe your sister didn't even write any book at all. And how do we know she died of natural causes? Now just what is your game?"

"Reginald, don't badger the poor girl. You'll

only make her forget more," the lady in lace intervened. "Now, my dear, can you remember where you were when she gave you the manuscript? Were you in front of the theatre or backstage?"

"No, Mum. I were in my lady's dressin' room, like always." Millie sniffed loudly into a large white handkerchief. "That's where I always worked when she was on stage, keeping everything nice for her the way she liked it. Always a fresh brewed cup of tea between acts. I always did it just right . . . "

Millie dissolved in tears, and Evan tugged at Elizabeth's arm. "Want to go talk to Nigel with me?"

"Sure, just as soon as I get one more cake. Did you have one of the chocolate ones?"

"Yeah, they're great!" They each took two more of the tempting cakes, then cornered Nigel in a large, overstuffed chair.

"What sort of arrangements did you make for your guests' comfort?"

"Did you tell your servants to stay in York?"

"Did you try to get a message through to the police?"

Evan's list of questions went on, and Elizabeth was impressed with the original thinking behind most of them.

"Did you plan the menu for the dinner?"

"My housekeeper oversees such matters."

Nigel brushed the insignificant matter off with a wave of his hand.

"But did you order the almond soup?" Evan persisted.

"Nasty stuff." Nigel made a face. "Ground almonds don't actually get creamy, you know, it's like eating bits of sand."

"You're not answering my question." Evan raised his voice. "Did you order cream of almond soup to hide the smell of cyanide? Or in hopes Gloria would choke on a bit of almond?"

"Actually, I think Gloria asked for that particular dish. It was a favorite of hers."

"That's a lie, it is!" Everyone turned in surprise to see that Millie had joined their group. "She 'ated almonds. If she ate any soup at all it was just one spoonful to be polite."

"Well, somebody told me she liked it."

Millie answered back angrily, and the interview showed lamentable signs of deteriorating into a shouting match. Elizabeth and Evan moved away.

"Say, how about the new actor, that Scotland Yard fellow? I wonder if anyone's thought to interview him?" Elizabeth said.

Evan looked at the man standing by Brian's elbow, trying to look inconspicuous. "What a good idea!"

Scott of the Yard wasn't unwilling to answer their questions, but he was a man of few words.

"Can you tell us what Mr. Rielly is charged with?" Elizabeth asked.

"No charge, Ma'am. Number 10 wants him for routine questioning."

"Have you been on this case long?"

"No, Ma'am."

Evan tried, "Have you made other arrests in connection with this case?"

"No, sir."

Elizabeth tried to think of something. Either there were no clues here or they were on entirely the wrong track.

"Will you be making other arrests while you're here?" she tried.

"Couldn't say, Ma'am."

Elizabeth sighed, and she and Evan exchanged looks of mutual frustration. Neither of them could think of anything more to ask, so they started to back off when Millie approached tearfully. "They're makin' the most 'orrible accusations. You tell 'em I wouldn't do no wrong," she pleaded to the officer.

"Now, Millie, calm down." His reply was in the same clipped monotone of all his answers, but it had an unusually soothing effect on Millie.

Elizabeth frowned at the scene in front of her, then asked, "You two know each other?"

"Of course, this 'eres my Uncle Scottie."

Uncle? Elizabeth couldn't remember why that rang a bell, but she turned back through her notes. "Oh, the uncle who helped Vicky go to night school?"

"Course 'e is. 'E's the only uncle I got, isn't 'e?"

"Is that right, sir?" Evan asked.

"Not to put too fine a point on it, I'd be stepuncle to Millie. She and Vicky had the same mother. Vicky's father was my brother."

A lightbulb went off in Elizabeth's head. "Ah, so you had more interest in this case than just the security risk."

"That's as may be, Ma'am."

"Do you know anything about the book Vicky wrote?"

"I gave her a few hints about how things work at the Yard."

"But you didn't read the manuscript?"

"Not that I'm sure of, Ma'am."

Elizabeth stopped her notetaking, "What do you mean, not sure?"

"I never read Vicky's story. But I read another with certain similarities to some ideas Vicky and I discussed, if you take my meaning." His glance at Linden Leigh, just rising from signing his last autograph, was more meaningful than the inspector's words.

Elizabeth looked at Lord Leigh open-mouthed. *"Clouds of Carcasses!"*

"What's that?" Leigh put his glass in his eye. "You want me to sign another autograph? Terribly sorry not to oblige, a spot of writer's cramp, old girl."

"I think a spot of writer's cribbing was more what the inspector was getting at."

"Oh, I say, that sounds frightfully unsporting."

"If not downright illegal, sir." Inspector Scott frowned at Sir Linden.

"I say, are you casting aspersions, old chap?" Leigh's voice became a shade darker.

"I wouldn't say but what a certain best-selling book bore certain resemblances to the ideas my niece was working with."

"Oh, yes, I see your point." Sir Linden smiled broadly. "But speak well of the dead and all that. The child was a good secretary. You can't blame her for picking up a few tidbits around the office, now can you? Might not even have been conscious. After all, she typed my stuff all day then went home to work on her own—most natural thing in the world if a few ideas just sort of stuck."

"So that's the way it is, is it, sir?" the inspector didn't return Sir Linden's smile.

"I'm certain it was. After all, she couldn't have hoped to get away with plagiarizing me. And first works tend to be highly eclectic." He turned from the inspector and offered his arm to Elizabeth. "I say, care for a stroll?" Elizabeth abandoned all ideas of questioning Bill Johnson and took Gavin's arm. He gave the others a jaunty wave. "Cheerio!"

Since the weather wouldn't permit an outdoors ramble, they just walked slowly down the corridor, up a flight of stairs, and along the hall to one of the secluded little alcoves. It was wonderful to be quiet after the crush of the autograph party and histrionics of the role-playing suspects. But Elizabeth's heart wasn't quiet; it was shouting hosannas and clapping for joy. It was with its beloved.

The nook they had chosen was furnished with a small, soft Chesterfield rather than the hard, uncomfortable Victorian sofas so prevalent in the old castle. Elizabeth leaned into the rounded corner. "Do you have trouble shifting back and forth from one persona to the other?"

"I'd hate to do this for a living. I think the role-playing here is worse that way than stage work would be, because the roles intermingle with everyday living. Like I was signing autographs as Gavin Kendall while talking to the inspector as Linden Leigh. It seems to take everyone that way. One lady asked me to sign her copy of *Clouds of Carcasses,* and no one seems sure whether to call me Sir Gavin or Sir Linden, so I just answer to both."

"Having your fictional character modeled so closely on your real life probably makes it harder, too."

"Makes the reality-acting line blur more, yes. But then I'm never stuck for an answer because I can always dig up a line from real life if something comes up that Stark hasn't prepped us ahead on."

"Does he give it all to you in a lot of detail?"

"He did this scenario with a fine-toothed comb, but there are still unforeseen things—" He took her hand—"like this . . . "

Her response to his kiss said everything she wanted to tell him but couldn't put into words. It was her apology for doubting him, it was her statement of trust, it was her pledge for the future. A future that could encompass all her dreams.

"Oooh, is that part of the script?" A passerby awoke Elizabeth to the fact that they were in a public room.

"Looks like we've got a new suspect to interview."

"And his fiancée not yet cold in the grave."

"Did you kill Gloria Glitz so you could marry Sir Linden?"

Speechless, Elizabeth blushed, but Gavin rose to the occasion. "An old friend, comforting me in my bereavement and all that. So you run along like good children and let her get on with it, what?"

They laughed and waved. "Sorry to interrupt."

"But we couldn't overlook any clues, you know."

Elizabeth gave a sigh of relief when their backs disappeared around the corner. "I guess that makes me Lady Leila what's-her-name?"

Gavin started. "How did you know?"

"About Lady Leila? You mentioned her in an

interview—old, old friend of the family, girlfriend before Gloria. Forgotten your own lines?"

"Forgotten my own ad-libbing—that's one of those items Stark hadn't choreographed. Bad form not to make up a name, though. Must respect the lady's privacy and all that."

"You mean there is a Lady Leila?"

"Yes, old friend, just like I said."

The information was strangely upsetting to Elizabeth. She turned away from Gavin.

"I say, there's nothing in it, you know. I don't deny there might have been at one time. But that's long past."

"No, it isn't that." She twisted her hands together, then brushed her hair back from her face. "At least, I don't think it is. I don't know— I just don't seem to be coping too well. I don't know what's real and what isn't. And just when I think I have it sorted out the edges of my nice tidy boxes start crumbling again."

Gavin stood and held his hand out to help her up. "But that's the problem; you can't put people in boxes. They will break out." He started walking her to her room. "Even in real life, how do you know when people you meet are being really honest or playing a part?" They were both silent for a moment. "I wonder how often they know themselves?"

But when they entered the parlor on Elizabeth's floor, there was no question that it was all reality. Two blue-uniformed policemen, with a great deal of mud splattered on their trousers, were directing crisp questions at Richard, who was explaining how they found the deceased's belongings, while Anita stood there with her notebook open.

"And this is the lady that discovered the body?" An officer turned to Elizabeth and opened a new page in his notebook.

They took Elizabeth's statement, then requested Gavin's passport and asked him all the same questions. "I think that'll be all for now. When we get a report from the lab there may be more questions."

"You're taking—er, Mr. Parkerson down to Hidden Glenn, are you?" Elizabeth asked.

"That's right. Coroner's men are there now. They'll have to carry him down the hill, though. Weather's still too rough to land a helicopter on this mountain."

"When will the road be cleared?" Richard asked.

"Soon. Maybe even tomorrow. Next day for sure, if no more mud comes down."

"Isn't that ironic," Elizabeth said. "Just the time they get the road clear, the police come in and tell everyone we can't go anyplace."

"I'm afraid that's about right." The taller of the two officers tipped his cap at her.

"You do think you'll find who did it, don't you?"

"Coming in so late after the fact doesn't help matters any. But since we've had a more-or-less captive audience here, I should think it'll be all right."

"And the jewels?" Richard asked.

"If they're here we should find them. If the thief made off over the mountain, that'll make it more difficult."

"Yes, well, good luck. Let us know if we can be of any more assistance." Gavin remarked.

Richard walked Anita to the doorway. "I do hope they recover your evening bag; it sounds very special."

"It was. Thank you, Richard. You've been a fantastic help." Anita went out.

"I didn't know she was robbed, too," Elizabeth said. "An evening bag? I thought they took only jewels."

"This was jeweled—a gold bag shaped like a cat with a diamond collar and emerald eyes."

"Sounds exotic—" At the sound of footsteps in the hall Elizabeth quit talking and looked out to watch the zipped up, white plastic body bag carried by. "I feel like I should put my hand over my heart, or cross myself, or something." She turned slowly back to the room.

Murmuring something about seeing them at dinner, Gavin left, and Elizabeth and Richard went to their rooms. Elizabeth realized she had never felt less like dressing for dinner in her life. But her wardrobe plan told her that tonight she was to wear the gown she thought of as her Ginger Rogers dress. Made of midnight blue Qiana, a crepelike material, the skirt flared and swirled around her feet when she walked, and the slim long sleeves ended in great ruffs of blue feathers.

She began feeling better as she slipped three long ropes of crystals around her neck and pinned a blue feather in her hair. When she entered the dining room with Richard, who looked tall and elegant in his black tie and tux, she was glad she had forced herself to the effort, especially when first Bill Johnson, then a lady from another table asked to take their picture. "Such a beautiful couple you make," the woman gushed, her bright pink boa tangling in the camera strap.

Now that the final interviews were finished, the intensity of the debate over who murdered Gloria Glitz increased to fever pitch, leaving room for hardly any interest in the fact that the police were there to investigate the jewel robbery.

Apparently Mr. Hamlin had persuaded the authorities to keep the fact of the murder quiet, or maybe the police weren't ready to say anything yet until the coroner's report was in. Either way, as soon as the players had found that the uniformed officers among them were for real and had no bearing on the mystery plot, they had given them little attention.

Elizabeth ate quietly, not really following the argument since she hadn't settled the question of guilt in her own mind. "Yoo-hoo, Elizabeth, are you home?" Irene snapped her fingers in front of Elizabeth. "I said, are you going to the video-tape showing of *The Moving Finger?*"

"Sorry. Obviously I was daydreaming. No, I don't think I will. That's my favorite Christie, but I'm unbelievably tired. I think I'll just read for awhile. Maybe take a nice long bath."

"That does sound appealing," Irene agreed. "But you might miss a clue."

Elizabeth laughed. "There's an incredible amount of Type A behavior going on around here. Don't these people realize they're supposed to be on vacation?"

"But mysteries aren't any fun if they don't get ahold of you. Who wants to read a thriller you can put down?"

"Well, just so they keep things in perspective and don't come to blows." Elizabeth looked at Evan, who was shaking a fist at Cathy, and she was surprised at the vehemence with which Helen was speaking to Benton on the other side of the table.

"How's the skit coming?" She turned back to Irene.

"I rounded up some artistic help from Helen and Cathy this afternoon. We have the puzzle all planned out, we just don't know whose face to put on it. We'll have to decide in the morning."

"Well, maybe I can get a nice long night of sleep and dream up the solution—something that will make everyone happy."

"Or all equally unhappy." Irene shrugged. "See you in the library after breakfast." She waved as Elizabeth rose to leave.

Richard started to get up, but she shook her head and signaled for him to stay seated. She really wanted to be alone. Irene's mention of the library had reminded her of the magazine item she wanted to look up.

It was on the top of the stack, just as Irene had said, and the picture was indeed very moving. Margo Lovell's face didn't show, but her black-veiled golden blond hair gleamed above the simple black mourning dress, and the slump to the shoulders and bent back of the kneeling figure spoke grief as clearly as only one with years of dramatic experience could communicate.

The bronze casket was draped with boughs of white flowers, and a Union Jack hung from a standard near the head of the coffin. The story below the picture referred to James Lovell's years of service as permanent secretary to a prominent minister of the crown and Lovell's tragic death when a terrorist bomb, undoubtedly intended for the minister, ended a fishing expedition in the lake district.

Elizabeth sat staring at the picture, wondering how much this woman had meant to Gavin.

Had he been as heartbroken at her death as she had been at her uncle's? Could she, Elizabeth, take this woman's place in his life? The library was quiet and her chair comfortable . . .

She started from a light doze when the magazine slid to the floor . . . *but someone said Gloria was marrying Leigh for his money and title—that must be nonsense, her own family held a position of importance* . . .

She picked up the magazine with a cry of frustration—it had happened again! The lines of reality had blurred on her, but this time the experience left her not just feeling baffled and disoriented. This time she felt the cold prickles of fear.

12

And all her oppressors themselves shall fade as a dream, a vision of the night." *Fade as a dream* . . . Elizabeth couldn't sort out why she was fearful or why that long-ago memorized verse from Isaiah 29 was so comforting, but all the way back to her room she kept saying it over and over, clinging to it to keep the shadows from falling across her path and tripping her.

" . . . fade as a vision of the night . . . "

The shadow that had fallen across her intermingling of dream and reality in the library had indeed been a vision of the night—a night in which truth and fiction were one and the reality of the whispered truth was unacceptable. But the shadow was so illusory. She needed a firm analysis of the situation, but she couldn't get hold of the image. The shadow kept falling between the idea and the reality.

She couldn't remember ever being happier to see anyone than she was when she walked into their parlor and found Richard sitting there. "Oh, I'm so glad you're here!" She flung out her arms to encompass the warmly lighted room as well as the man sitting before the fire crackling on the hearth. She had come in out of the night and the oppressing shadows had fled. She had come home.

Richard rose and came to her. "You look upset."

"I was, but I'm not sure why. Just tired, I expect."

He took her hands. "You're cold, too. Come sit by the fire and get warm." He pulled her to the sofa and sat beside her.

"Did you have a nice evening?" she asked.

"Yes, I did." The sound of his deep voice was so comforting, she wanted him just to keep talking.

"Anita seems like a really nice person—"

"Anita is an absolute darling. I will always be thankful you talked me into com—"

Suddenly Gavin exploded into the room. "On your balcony! Did you see him?" he said urgently to Elizabeth.

They rushed to her room, looking toward the curtained glass door between two windows. The shade on the nearest window was only partly drawn. Against the black sky she could see the skeletal outline of the iron railing along one side of the balcony, but no figure was visible.

"I'm sure it was your balcony. I just glanced out the window along the corridor." Gavin crossed the room and yanked the balcony door open. "There he goes!"

Richard dashed after Gavin into the night.

Elizabeth shivered from the blast of cold air, then ran after the men just in time to see Richard climb over the rail and drop to the balcony below. "Be careful!" The wind blew her words back in her face.

Gripping the cold metal bar she leaned over into the blank space, suspended four stories from the ground against the side of a stone building. She heard scuffling and male voices somewhere below, but she could see only darkness.

Oh, God keep him safe. Help him. Her mind swam with shadowy images of feet slipping on cold metal, an evil hand clutching a throat . . . *No, God! Don't let it happen. Help!* . . . A glint of cold light on the blade of a knife, a body falling through space . . . *God, God, do something!*

Far below she heard the thud of a person dropping to the ground, then running feet. This time her imaginings were of someone falling over rocky ground, a body lying broken and bloody on the boulders. *No, God, help him!* Then the figure was running again, but the pursuer had become the pursued and her mind drew the picture of a gun—a handful of death encased in blue-black steel. *Oh, God, God!*

She huddled in a corner of the balcony, her back against the cold stone, and sank to the floor with noiseless sobs. *God, help me think.* But the verses that came to her, Isaiah 21:3-4, only increased her horror: "I am distraught past hearing, dazed past seeing, my mind reels, sudden convulsions seize me. The cool twilight I longed for has become a terror."

She didn't know how long she crouched there in a heap until Richard came to take her in. "Richard! You're safe! And Gavin?"

"He's fine. Went to tell the police what happened." He led Elizabeth to the parlor and drew her close to the fire, keeping his arm around her for warmth.

"What did happen?"

"Nothing. Fellow got clean away. But he must have left a trail in this mud." He glanced at his own brown-caked shoes. "I suppose the police can follow it in the morning."

"By then it'll be too late," she said.

"Probably. But unless he intends to walk clear to Manitou Springs he'll have to surface someplace in the valley."

"Well, that probably means the jewels are gone. I had hoped to get grandmother's brooch back—it's mostly sentiment, but . . . I suppose the really valuable stuff was insured . . . " She buried her head against the warm shoulder holding her; she didn't want to babble on about jewels and robberies. "Oh, I'm so thankful you're safe—both of you. I was so scared. I prayed and prayed. But it was awful. The only verse I could think of was all about anguish and terror. It was like God was mocking me."

"Elizabeth . . . " For an instant she thought she felt his lips on her hair. Then he moved to seat her on the sofa and picked up his Bible, which he'd left there earlier. "What was it, do you know?"

"Isaiah, I think. Twenty-one, maybe."

He turned the pages and scanned the passage silently, then nodded slowly. "Yes, I see. But God wasn't mocking you. He was telling you he understood. 'My limbs writhe in anguish, I am gripped by pangs like a woman in labor . . . ' From the beginning of time people have suffered, and they always will. And he will always suffer right along with them."

Elizabeth's face relaxed in a smile. "Yes, I see. Oh, that helps so much."

Richard turned back several pages. "Now, let's try something different. Read this." He handed her the Bible open to Psalm Twenty-Seven, his finger on the fifth verse.

She read: "'For he will keep me safe beneath his roof in the day of misfortune . . . he will raise me beyond reach of distress.'" She put the book down, "'Beyond reach of distress,' that's beautiful! Thank you so much, Richard. What would I do without you?"

"I had hoped you wouldn't have to find out."

She turned away, unable to meet his level look.

He took her face between his hands and turned her gently back to him. She raised her eyes to his face; what she saw written there stopped her heart. "Richard, I . . . No! I'm so sorry, Richard. I thought you were over that . . . " But she couldn't turn away. So she took his hand in hers and kissed his palm before she dropped it.

He was the one to turn. "Yes, well—I'll just have to try harder to get over it, won't I? Don't worry, Elizabeth. One does get over things. Some of us just bleed longer and heal slower, that's all."

An uncontrollable shiver shook her. Richard turned back to her. "Elizabeth, you got chilled out there on the balcony. Into a nice hot tub with you. And stay there until you're warm through." He gave her a gentle shove toward her room.

The bathroom quickly filled with steam as the hot water gushed from the tap, churning Elizabeth's bath beads into a froth of bubbles. She took a deep breath of the fresh herbal scent. This was just what she needed. She hated the quickie showers the frenzied tempo of the week had required.

Her body relaxed in the delicious warmth, but her heart still felt constricted. She cared so much for Richard, longed to comfort him and fill his needs. And it would be such a logical thing to do, so simple. "Yes, Richard." Just two words—that's all she would have to say. Why did love have to be so illogical and disruptive?

She thought back over the scene in front of the fire. Was it significant that neither Gavin nor Anita had been mentioned? She had wanted to, but the words wouldn't come out. The things between her and Richard concerned no third or fourth parties—no outsiders.

She languidly scooped a handful of bubbles and blew at them, reveling in her warm, bright comfort. Then she thought of the contrast of those awful moments, or hours, however long it had been, cold and dark on the balcony—the terror of the dark of night and the worse darkness of not knowing what was happening below her. *Thank you, Lord, for keeping him safe.*

Then it occurred to her to ask herself who "he" was. For whom had she been praying?

Well, both of them, of course, she replied with quick defensiveness. But honesty required her to admit that each time her prayer had been help *him,* not help them. Had the picture in her mind held a man with dark brown hair or blond?

She shifted uneasily in the tub, then realized her discomfort was more than just mental—what was she sitting on? Putting a hand under her hips, she ran her finger over the bottom of the tub. Oh, those rubber flowers they put on to keep one from slipping and having a nasty fall in the tub. Then, as her finger traced the five-petaled flower shape, she froze. She had seen a similar pattern before.

Maybe not. Maybe it wasn't the same. Moving slowly, dreading what she might find, she ran her hand down the back of her thigh—one flower petal under her leg.

Her hand stopped, as if it refused to obey the orders from her mind to explore further. Was she the same height as the corpse? She looked at her feet snug against the front of the tub in her reclining position . . . *Go on!* she ordered. She had to know, had to make certain beyond any doubt . . .

She stretched out her arm and reached across to her left leg. It was there, just as she knew it would be.

No. It can't be. Don't let me be right. If Parkerson was dead when she first saw him in her tub—and the blood settling in his body stamped this indelible evidence, then the possible answers to the question of who moved the body were severely limited.

Who had known about her discovery? Dr. Pearsall, whose actions she had considered suspicious earlier. Presumably, he could have moved the corpse while the others were busy, could have said he wanted a quiet word with him, or wanted to examine him or something. That

THE CASTLE OF DREAMS

would make sense if the doctor and Hamlin were conspirators.

It seemed to clear Bill Johnson and Anita of her suspicions. Unless she had been unconscious longer than she realized and more people had come into her suite than she knew. But surely someone would have mentioned it.

Then an entirely new idea struck her. Weldon Stark—the man who had been 'calling the shots' all week, the man who had choreographed everything. Gavin said Stark had first claimed Parkerson as a member of the acting company, then later denied it. Just what was Stark's involvement?

Or was he involved at all? She had only Gavin's word to go on . . .

Gripping the side of the tub, she pulled herself out and forced herself to dry off and get dressed before phoning Richard. But then her hand froze in midmotion . . . Richard had backed up everything Gavin said. Or had Gavin backed up Richard's words? What was actually said? Why couldn't she remember? She had never doubted one word from either of them. Could they have done it together? Who could she trust? Where would the policemen be at this hour of the night?

No, no, NO! Going to the police with suspicions about Richard—and Gavin, she added hurriedly—was absolutely ridiculous. There had to be a logical explanation. Whatever had happened—and her mind filled with unlikely and unsavory scenarios—whatever it was, there had to be a reasonable answer.

She dialed Richard's room, speaking the moment he answered. "Richard! Would you please come to my room for a moment?" She thought she kept the agitation out of her voice, but the speed with which Richard responded indicated that her alarm was apparent. Or was he waiting for her—knowing what she was likely to find in the tub?

"Elizabeth," he said as she let him in, "what now? You're trembling."

Without replying she stepped into the bathroom to the tub and pulled the plug on the drain. In a few moments she pointed to the raised rubber flowers with a few soap bubbles still clinging to them. "Do you recognize that?"

Richard's sharp intake of breath told her that, indeed, he did. She watched his features carefully to see if he betrayed any look of guilt or conspiracy, but all she saw was open amazement as he knelt by the tub and traced the pattern with his forefinger just as she had done earlier. "Parkerson."

Her voice was quiet with horror. "He was dead the first time." She couldn't look at him as she went on, "But, Richard, you said . . . You agreed it was part of the act . . . " She closed her eyes and turned away. It was the stupidest thing she could possibly do if Richard was involved.

But if that was the case, she would rather he just close his fingers tightly around her neck and end it. There was no way she could face the idea of Richard . . .

She trembled as his hands clasped her shoulders and moved upward toward her neck. Then she relaxed as he pulled her against him and led her into her sitting room. "Now think, Elizabeth. You regained consciousness on this sofa. What did I say?"

"You said the man was an actor, but Stark would call off that scenario."

"No. Gavin said that—later. Now think. What was the first thing I said? When you first came to?"

She closed her eyes, remembering. "You said Gavin sent the man away, and you got the doctor."

"That's right. I rushed out immediately for Dr. Pearsall. When we arrived back here Gavin said he had told the fellow off and got rid of him."

"Richard." Now her eyes were open wide with horror. "Isn't there some other possibility?"

"Like?"

"Like rubber flowers in other tubs—probably every tub in the hotel—"

Richard didn't reply.

"Well," her voice was sharp and high-pitched. "It's possible."

Richard nodded slowly. "I think that's an assessment the police should make."

"Richard, no! Please, Richard."

"I've never known you to be foolish before, Elizabeth."

"OK, maybe I am . . . I don't know. But please give me a little time to work through this myself. I mean, there are police all over the hotel now; surely waiting a little while won't matter."

"All right—but I'm certain you're making a mistake."

She held her ground, in spite of the cold shiver that shook her.

13

Saturday

Elizabeth took the last of Dr. Pearsall's little blue pills that night, so she slept through breakfast and arrived at the Blithe Spirit meeting the next morning feeling anything but blithe.

But then, the team spirit in the library could hardly be called blithe, either.

"I think we should do a seance; it's such a natural with our name. Madame Arcati could conduct it."

"It is a natural, but it's been done before. Matter-of-fact, last year's winning team did a seance."

"Which one are we going for, the accuracy prize or the originality prize?"

"We won't be going for either one if we can't settle on who the murderer is. Now, look, Nigel Cass had the most opportunity—"

Evan waved his notebook at his father. "No, Dad, it was a conspiracy between Susie and

Brian. That's the only logical explanation for her confession."

"But Nigel—"

"I agree with you both, partially," Benton broke in with the authority of his legal training. "It was a conspiracy, but you've got the wrong players, Evan. It was Nigel and Millie. Then she wanted out of the deal, and that's why he tried to get rid of her."

"That's too complicated," Anita objected. "I think Millie acted alone."

"No, Brian acted alone—a spy wouldn't need an accomplice." Cathy's cheeks flushed red in her excitement.

"Susie acted alone to protect her lover," Mrs. Johnson spoke with decision.

"Well, I personally think Gavin did it because he seems the least likely," Irene said lightly. "But please, just settle on someone so we can get to work!"

"I told you, Nigel—"

"No way, Susie and Brian—"

"You guys are crazy, Millie—"

Irene broke into the dispute, "Come on, Elizabeth, your vote breaks the deadlock."

"Yeah, you haven't said anything yet."

"No chickening out!"

"Right, name your villain."

Elizabeth squirmed at the silence in the room as everyone waited for her answer. "I don't know . . . have we established it was murder? It looked so natural. Some of you thought it was a real choking at first."

"Has to be murder," Benton said. "Without a villain the whole mystery's pointless."

"Right." Elizabeth hesitated. "But I . . . I can't make hard decisions on an empty stomach." She hoped they'd let her get off with a joke.

"OK, you've got until after lunch," Bill Johnson said, and the others agreed. They were serious; they weren't letting her out of this.

"I've got an appointment after lunch. Er, for a sauna and massage," Anita said quickly. "I can't come back."

"Yeah, and we were going for a hike. Since the rain finally stopped it's our only chance to get out," Evan spoke for his whole family.

"Well, I—uh . . . ," " Elizabeth stuttered.

"OK, young lady," Benton said. "Take all the time and food you need. I move we elect Elizabeth our official jury chairperson. Whatever she decides, we'll all go with. And no complaining afterwards."

"But what if we don't agree with her?" Evan asked.

"That's the point," Benton replied. "We've had all week to come to an agreement and failed. So we'll elect a spokesman and be done."

"Elizabeth's the perfect one. Since she isn't propounding a theory she'll be more objective," Helen said.

"Good idea! I agree." Anita picked up her purse with an air of finality.

"All in favor say, 'aye,'" Benton said.

The room reverberated with ayes.

"The ayes have it. Good luck, Elizabeth. Whatever you say, we'll go with it and no complaints—whatever the outcome."

Everyone started toward the door. "Wait!" Irene held up her hands. "Elizabeth, let me know as soon as you can who to put on the puzzle. We'll meet here after tea to practice. Right?"

Everyone agreed and escaped to freedom. Everyone but Elizabeth, who now had to deal with the full weight of her conscience. If she was to do an honest job, she would be forced to think through what she was trying so hard to avoid—to face the suspicion that had been growing steadily in her mind all week. She turned at the sound of a footstep entering the room. "Richard, where have you been? Why weren't you here to bail me out? I've been stuck with deciding for the whole team."

"Know what you're going to say?"

She shook her head and looked at the floor.

"It's a tough one, isn't it?"

"Richard! You could do it. I was only elected because I happened to be here. You could decide."

He looked at her intently. "Could I? Can anyone really decide this but you, Elizabeth?" She knew he was referring to far more than her answer to a game. "Two things I can do for you," he said as he offered his arm to lead her from the room. "Feed you and pray for you."

Elizabeth was less than halfway through her fruit salad and cinnamon roll when Weldon Stark, Mr. Hamlin, and a police officer went to the microphone on the dais. Stark spoke first. "The bad news is that all you amateur sleuths have been left in the shade by the professionals. The good news is that Detective Foster and his men have recovered the stolen jewels." Applause and cries of joy accompanied his announcement. He held up his hand for silence. "The bad news is that the thief has not yet been apprehended. The good news is that the officers believe the robbery was the work of an amateur and should not be hard to track."

Mr. Hamlin started to speak, but was met with cries of, "Where were the stolen goods?" "How did you find them?" "Tell us about it!" from the hotel guests. So the manager surrendered the mike to Detective Foster.

"When a search of the grounds revealed no footprints leaving the hotel, we were confident the jewels were hidden inside. We noticed in Mr. Hamlin's report of the robbery that most of the burglarized rooms were on the fourth floor, so my men did a routine search of that floor. The jewels were found in the crawl space behind a repair panel along the south corridor." A burst of applause interrupted his speech. Officer Foster grinned at the accolade. "We find that it's hard to beat good routine police work, even if it sometimes lacks the flair and excitement of your Sherlock Holmes or Nero Wolfes." The audience laughed and applauded again.

Mr. Hamlin started to take the mike again, but there were still unanswered questions: "Why do you say it was the work of an amateur?"

"A professional would have kept the jewels with him, and he would have chosen only the highest quality jewels to steal—this was a very mixed bag."

"If it wasn't a professional job, why do you think it was done?" came from the back of the room.

Officer Foster shrugged. "Maybe to add a little excitement to your week, maybe to create a diversion from something else, maybe to pick up what looked like easy money. Or, with jewels there's always the possibility of an insurance scam. When I said it was amateur work, I didn't mean it wasn't necessarily a real robbery. And Mr. Stark here assures me it was not part of his plot."

Stark nodded, and the hotel manager took the microphone for the third time to explain how the victims of the robbery could reclaim their property.

"Well, I say, that's good news." Sir Gavin joined the Blithe Spirit table and took an empty chair next to Elizabeth. After her doubts of the night before she started to recoil, but when she looked at him—looked in his clear blue eyes—it just seemed too ridiculous, no matter what the evidence of the tub seemed to say. "When you're through there I expect you'll want to toddle on down to the manager's office and collect Grandma's stickpin?"

"I certainly do." Elizabeth indulged in spreading butter on her cinnamon roll. "I'd like to stick it into the clown that stole it. It's the only piece of real jewelry I've ever owned—no matter what that Detective Foster may have meant about some of the loot being very poor quality." Then another thought struck her.

"But did you notice what he said about no tracks leading away from the hotel? What do you suppose happened to that man you and Richard chased last night?"

Gavin shrugged. "Could have doubled back into the hotel by a service door or something, or even gotten away on rocky ground that didn't leave any prints."

"But why didn't he take the jewels with him?"

"Probably got cold feet and just decided to make a break for it. That fits with what the officer said about his being an amateur."

But would Scotland Yard track an amateur across the Atlantic?

Elizabeth couldn't find a voice to speak her doubts, so she let it drop and followed Gavin to the manager's office.

When Elizabeth had given her solemn statement to the officer on duty in Mr. Hamlin's
office and identified and signed for her family
heirloom, she pinned it firmly to the shoulder of
her soft white dress.

"Shall we celebrate its return with a stroll in
the sun?" Gavin suggested.

"Yes, I'd love to!" Elizabeth was embarrassed
when she heard the enthusiasm in her own voice.
It would be wonderful to get out in the fresh air
and sunshine, it would be a relief to be able to
postpone her decision for the team, it would be
lovely to be alone with Gavin . . . wouldn't it? At
least half of her was sure it would be and longed
to be in his arms as she was days ago when they
had walked to the gazebo. But the other half of
her was protesting loudly, *If you go with him,
you'll have to tell him what you found. Don't be a
dummy; tell the police.*

*Tell the police I suspect the man I love? And
when Gavin has a simple explanation for my
doubts, what will he think of me?*

But what do you think of Gavin? her mind
asked.

I love him, her heart replied.

The high mountain air was cool and the ground
underfoot squishy from days of rain soaking it,
but the sun was sparkling on the lake, and a few
birds were singing in the trees along the trail.
"Have you ever been to England?" Gavin asked.

"No, but I'd love to. Is it anything like this?"

"Well, I'll admit all the rain seemed familiar. Our mountains are nothing like this—not nearly so high and rugged. And our trees are largely deciduous." They walked on in silence for a few minutes, listening to the bird calls. Then Gavin turned to her. "Elizabeth, let me show it to you. Will you come to England with me?"

"Gavin . . . I . . . " Was this an invitation to take a tour? An illicit offer? Or a proposal of marriage? "I don't know what to say."

They were nearing the gazebo where he first kissed her, where she first felt their hearts become one. Would he stop there again? Did she want him to? She hated the confusion that plagued her. Her constant prayer was for God to lead her, to show her what was right. So why didn't he answer?

Around a bend in the trail, the gazebo came into view. Gavin put his finger to his lips and exaggerated walking quietly. One glance at the little wooden summer house told her why—a couple sat there locked in an embrace. An embrace that appeared to be as complete an experience as her time there with Gavin had been. Then, a few steps nearer and she realized—it was Richard and Anita.

When the gazebo was well behind them and they started around the far end of the lake, Gavin repeated his question, "I hate to make a nuisance of myself and all that, but do you think you could put up with me as a tour guide?"

"I'm sure you'd be an absolutely marvelous tour guide." Elizabeth laughed with relief at not having to answer a more difficult question.

Their path broke through the bushes and began climbing steeply toward the top of the quarry wall. "Well, now that's satisfactory. How about—"

Elizabeth took a deep breath and plunged. She had to have her questions answered before she could answer him. "Gavin, I've got to talk to you about something. When Richard and I went back to look at Parkerson's body we found a strange mark—like a flower—on his bottom."

"A tattoo?"

The path reached its highest peak and followed right by the edge of the cliff.

"No. It was printed there by the way the blood settled after he—er, died." She couldn't bring herself to say "was killed." "Last night I discovered what made the mark . . . "

"Your bathtub?"

She stopped and gasped. He admitted it? She had hoped and prayed it somehow wasn't true, but he knew all along. With a small moan she stepped backward, nearer the edge of the drop-off. Suddenly, Gavin's features twisted and contorted.

Elizabeth stepped on a small rock, and her foot slipped. His hands came out at her. It couldn't have lasted more than a fraction of a second, but in that dot of time as he reached for her she envisioned the terrifying horror of falling through blank space, her own voice screaming in her ears as her body fell faster than the sound past the jagged knifeblades of cut granite, the scream echoing from each rock until she broke through the rain-swollen surface of the inky water, then falling slower and slower until she could fall no more . . .

"Hello there!"

"We thought we heard your voices."

Gavin's hands closed on her arm and pulled her back from the edge of the precipice as Richard and Anita approached. "Careful! You were right on the edge. You could have gone over." Gavin held her securely to him, and she felt his heart beating as wildly as her own.

"Uh-oh, looks like we're interrupting, Richard," Anita said.

"Good thing you did." Gavin still held Elizabeth. "This silly girl was about to back off the cliff. Devilishly cold weather for a swim, what?"

"Well, take care of her, Kendall, or I'll hold you responsible." Richard spoke lightly, but he gave Gavin a level look before leading Anita on along the trail.

"I say, that was a bit fright-making. You're still trembling. There's another one of these gazebo things just up here. Let's sit."

Inside the little wooden pagoda, he tried to

put his arm around her again, but she pulled away with a shake of her head. She sat with her head in her hands, her eyes closed, trying to remember, trying to forget—trying to think, trying to blot out everything.

But Gavin's voice penetrated her muddle, "Right. We need to talk. Yes, the poor chap was dead the first night and, of course, I knew he wasn't part of Stark's scenario because we had rehearsed it all the day before. But you were so thoroughly upset, and I knew nothing could be done until the landslide was cleared away. So I suggested Richard run for the doctor, and I took our unwelcome guest next door and, er, put him to bed, as you might say. There was no need to perturb anyone further, there had been quite enough excitement already that night."

To Elizabeth the smooth logic of his answer was more confusing than ever. He always had a perfect answer. Would she be gullible to believe him, or horrible to suspect him? She just shook her head.

"Take me back, Gavin," she said, her voice as flat as her feelings. "I need to think."

14

These are the words of the Holy One of Israel: . . . . You shall weep no more. The Lord will show you favor and answer you when he hears your cry for help. . . . If you stray from the road to right or left you shall hear with your own ears a voice behind you saying, This is the way; follow it."

Elizabeth's bed creaked under her as she leaned over to put her Bible on the table just half an hour after Gavin brought her back. The words from Isaiah 30 kept running through her head, and she sighed. "OK, Lord, you promised. I am crying for your help, so show me the way."

She picked up her notebook. She flipped to the back where she had listed events and clues that made two complete, perfectly logical scenarios. Well, almost complete. Each would make a good skit and fulfill her obligation to

Blithe Spirit. One was fun, lighthearted, and safe. The other was heavy, deadly serious, and possibly dangerous. Could she do it? Could she not do it? Could she stay in her rosy dream world? Or must she reach out for the cold light of reality?

"This is the way; walk ye in it."

Yes, Lord.

"You shall know the truth and the truth shall make you free."

Yes, Lord.

She took the cap off her pen and began writing the script.

When Elizabeth arrived at the library with ink-stained fingers, Irene was already organizing her cast. "Now, when the narration refers to something that was heard the ears will come forward and dance like this—" She demonstrated, then walked Bill and Helen, holding blank puzzle pieces, through the paces. "Now, eyes—Evan and Cathy—you go like this . . . then stand back here." She looked up and saw Elizabeth. "Ah, author! Author! Now we can get down to work. Here, Richard, you're the nose—"

"Typecasting, huh?" He touched his own long nose and everyone laughed.

Smiling, Irene handed a piece to Anita. "After that, I'm scared to tell you you're the mouth."

"Oh, that'd suit any woman." Bill ducked as his wife tried to hit him.

"OK, then I'll come in with the hair, and Dad, you complete the picture with the frame."

"Hey," Evan quipped, "we want the real solution, not a frame-up."

"I've got the real solution," Elizabeth said quietly. She stood by the side of the imaginary stage to read her script while Irene directed the puzzle pieces through her choreography.

When the skit was complete the players stood looking at Elizabeth with their mouths open:

"Wow! I didn't see that!"

"That's good."

"I think you've got it."

"It's awfully involved, but it makes sense," Anita said.

"Yes." Elizabeth's answer was barely audible.

"Are you sure?" Richard touched her elbow.

"No."

"Why did you take it on so far?" Irene asked.

Elizabeth's answer was to Richard rather than to Irene, "Because I have to be sure."

"I just heard," Richard said so only Elizabeth could hear, "the coroner ruled death by asphyxiation—smothered."

"How do you know?"

"Er, an officer told me."

"OK," Irene clapped her hands for attention. "Let's run through this again, then we'll just have time to go dress for 'le big event' tonight. You're looking good already, you guys. I want you to relax and have fun with this. Places, every-body . . . "

"I have never before seen this amount of glitter in one place in my life." Richard stood in the doorway with Elizabeth surveying the dining parlor an hour later. The Grand Soirée was the climax party of the week, and the room shimmered and glowed with the light reflected from the draped satin lamé and glittering sequins of the women's gowns. Each table was mounded with pink and white silver-spangled carnations, while opalescent balloons floated above the flickering tapers in the centerpieces. Dim lights in the high ceiling gave the effect of stars. Elizabeth's gown was a float of cerise chiffon with butterfly sleeves that matched the luster of the evening. An intricate pattern of gold beadwork scrolled down the front. Richard looked at her and smiled gently. "You outshine them all." He rested his hand briefly on her shoulder before offering his arm to escort her into the room.

When she moved her head, a cluster of gold bangles hanging from a headband glimmered in her dark hair. "Thank you." She smiled up at him. "It feels trite to say a man in white tie and tails looks splendid, but you really do. There's no other word for it."

Then Sir Gavin Kendall approached and bowed over her hand, and other words did spring to mind: *elegant, noble,* and *one born to the tradition through generations of men who dressed for dinner nightly.*

An orchestra played at the far end of the room, and waiters moved smoothly between the tables carrying trays laden with lobster thermidore, chateaubriand, and asparagus hollandaise. The chatter around the table was animated; everyone was celebrating the evening and what they were sure would be the winning skit when they presented it tomorrow. Already plans were under way for next year: "If we tell the hotel ahead, we can all be on the same team together again."

"Yes, we must. It wouldn't be the same with other people."

"I wonder if Weldon Stark will direct it again?"

"I can't imagine anyone doing a better job."

"Rather sure of your solution, are you?" Gavin asked.

Elizabeth nodded. She was the only one not jubilant over her script. If only she could be sure. Probably every team in the room was equally certain of their own answer. But none of the others were working with anything but a fictional game—a romp of the imagination that they would leave behind them tomorrow afternoon, taking nothing more than a scrapbook of snapshots and some good conversation topics home with them.

But if Elizabeth was right, she would go

home with a mutilated heart and a lifetime of shredded dreams. She had to be sure. Deadly sure.

The waiter set a raspberry meringue surrounded with chocolate curls before Elizabeth, calling her back to the present. She looked around guiltily, hoping no one had been able to detect her thoughts. But the others' minds were happily on the revelry and good food around them.

The Scripture she had memorized from Isaiah 21 just three days before came to her as clearly as if the person sitting in the next chair had spoken: "The banquet is set out, the rugs are spread; they are eating and drinking—rise, princes, burnish your shields. . . . Go, post a watchman to report what he sees."

She repeated the words again in her mind, more slowly this time, letting them speak to her: *Go, post a watchman* . . . All right, that was what she was supposed to do. Now, how would she go about it?

"I say, I'm supposed to circulate—mingle with the common folk, what? Care to take a turn around the room with me?" Gavin was holding his eyeglass, getting into character.

Elizabeth swallowed her last raspberry. "Great. I'd love to get a better look at all the costumes."

"Will you excuse us?" Sir Gavin bowed to Helen Johnson.

"Certainly! Go take a stroll with your beautiful

lady." Helen blew a kiss at them, and Elizabeth felt anew the Cinderella quality of the evening.

The musicians struck up a lively tune, and several couples started toward the dance floor, which gave Elizabeth a perfect opportunity to enjoy the fashion parade. Now that she knew what she had to do, it was easier to relax and enjoy the gala evening.

Gavin stopped at each table, greeting players with whom he had become acquainted, complimenting women on their gowns and making witty comments. To Elizabeth, the laughter around her, the music from the orchestra, the glimmering lights, all blended and spun together with the dancing couples like a carousel.

Tomorrow's skit was forgotten as she let herself be swept up in the fantasy of the moment. As they strolled past the glowing fireplace, Gavin put his arm around her lightly and they were characters in a play—Romeo and Juliet at the Capulet ball, perhaps? That was before Romeo killed Tybalt . . .

The horror of the thought halted her steps. Juliet loved Romeo even after he killed her kinsman. If her suspicions were correct, could she . . . ?

They were close to the musicians' dais when the brass struck up a swinging version of "Chattanooga ChooChoo," and Gavin reacted with a frown. "I say, this is the third loud number in a row. It's giving me a beastly headache. Shall we step out on the balcony?"

The air was crisp, but without the chill of the night before. Here the music reached them at a comfortable level. Far below in the valley the lights of Hidden Glenn glimmered like silver sequins on a black velvet ball gown. "Elizabeth." She jumped at the intensity of Gavin's voice. The man beside her had suddenly shed his role-playing impersonations. He was completely Gavin Kendall, and he was totally, intently hers. "Elizabeth, we need to talk. Tomorrow all this will be over, and I think we both know we can't just shake hands and say, 'Good-bye, it's been fun.'

"Elizabeth, I love you. I've never felt like this about anyone before. I've done so many things in the past that I'm terribly ashamed of and sorry for, but with you I could make a whole new start—"

She started to speak, but he laid a finger on her lips to silence her. "I'm not asking for a life-time commitment. That wouldn't be at all fair when you've never even been to England. But will you at least promise to come over this summer—I'll send you a ticket—and you can take all the time you need to decide."

It was everything she had been waiting to hear all her life. With all her being she wanted to throw her arms around his neck and vow a thousand times that she'd come, that she didn't need to look things over or think any longer—she'd found him, and that was all she needed. She could just tell Irene in the morning that they were going to use the other script. No one would know. Except herself. And God.

"Ask me again tomorrow after the skits, Gavin." The pain she felt at saying those words was as great as if her heart were physically bleeding. If the answer in the skit was right, there would be no choice; if it was wrong, he wouldn't want her.

Now she had a job to do. "You see, I can't really think of anything else until that's over because the team put the whole responsibility on me, and I can't get it off my mind."

"Got it solved, have you? Good show."

She looked at him earnestly for a long time. "I know the real answer, Gavin. It's all in the script."

He nodded. "Shall we go in?"

She moved away from the wall so he could open the door. In all the time on the balcony, she had not gone near the railing.

Just inside the door they met Weldon Stark. He greeted Gavin warmly, then turned an appreciative gaze on Elizabeth.

"You've done a marvelous job running things this week," she said.

"Marvelous enough that you'd be willing to leave this bloke and dance with me?" Stark held out his hand.

This was just the opportunity she needed.

Elizabeth put her hand in his. At first she concentrated on the waltz steps. Stark was a wonderful dancer of the old school; he led firmly and included a little dip in his step. But once they reached the middle of the floor, Elizabeth reminded herself to get back on task. "Mr. Stark, I want to tell you about my script for our skit tomorrow . . . it's, er . . . something rather different."

He listened intently, and she felt his arms tighten around her as she went on. "A real murder, you're saying?" He missed a step, but recovered quickly. She nodded.

"Are you sure that's a good idea?"

"The script is in my room. It's all final."

Stark started to argue more, but the number ended, and he was claimed by the guest who was still wearing her pink feather boa, as she had to every event all week.

Elizabeth turned to find Dr. Pearsall and repeat her dialogue.

Richard was just turning out the lights in the sitting room when she came in.

"You left the party before the excitement. Have you heard?"

"What?"

"Scott of the Yard died."

"What!" This was too much. She couldn't cope with another catastrophe. Then she looked at Richard's grin. "Oh, you mean as part of the script."

"Of course. He got up to make some kind of an announcement, then keeled over very dramatically clutching his heart."

"So it looked like a heart attack—natural causes?"

"I suppose so, but who knows? Stark certainly knows how to keep the tension up through the eleventh hour."

"Hmmm. I'd give a lot to know if that was in his original plan or an improvisation." She stood there looking uncertain and trying to think until Richard yawned and turned toward his room.

She wished him a brief good night and went on into her own room. Moving with a sense of detached calm, she took off her flame red ball gown and put on three layers of the warmest clothes in her suitcase. Then she pulled the blanket off her bed, stuffing the covers with towels and folded clothing so that it would appear she was asleep. Then she tiptoed across the sitting room, repeating over and over to herself, "Go, post a watchman . . . go . . ."

Before stepping out onto the balcony she took one last look around the room: Script on the table, window shades at the right level . . . she closed the door behind her, wrapped herself in the blanket, and taking a position where she could see under the shade, began her lonely vigil.

At first the excitement of what she was doing

provided stimulation to keep her awake, but as the moments dragged on and the hotel behind her went to sleep and the lights in the valley below blinked off, she found it necessary to fight her own drowsiness. She didn't dare get up and move around, so she flexed her muscles in rotation and forced herself to breathe deeply of the fresh night air.

Singing was always a good way to keep oneself awake, but hardly appropriate for a secret stakeout. So she decided to try quoting Scripture. She would see if she could recall every verse she'd memorized in the past week. Her mind strained at the thought, but only snatches of the prophet's words would come to her: "All revelry is darkened, and mirth is banished. . . . desolation alone is left. . . ." "Whether they turn their gaze upwards or look down, everywhere is distress and darkness inescapable, constraint and gloom that cannot be avoided; for there is no escape . . ." With those words from Isaiah ringing in her mind, she turned her gaze upwards, then looked down—and everywhere was inescapable darkness. Her only comfort lay in Richard's words, "God is telling you he understands, that he is there with you."

As time wore on, Elizabeth shifted her position carefully to relieve muscles that were beginning to ache. Even as warmly as she was dressed, cold seeped in around the edges of the blanket. *This is really dumb, you know. You could be sound asleep in your nice warm bed right now—like Gavin and Stark and all your other imaginary bogey men are. You are being unbelievably idiotic—carried away by the aura of the mystery week and all the thrillers you've read. If you told your theory to an objective observer like a policeman he'd laugh you out of the room—or offer you first rights for a fiction publication.*

She was within inches of talking herself into standing up and chucking the whole thing when another verse, Isaiah 30:15, came to her mind: "Keep peace, and you will be safe; in stillness and in staying quiet, there lies your strength . . . Wait."

Yes, Lord, but how long?

She wrapped the blanket tighter around her, stifled a yawn that made her eyes water, and leaned her head back against the cold iron bars of the railing . . .

It was only the merest click, barely audible. She was sure her heart leaping into her throat made a far louder sound. But it was enough to call her back from the cloud she was drifting away on and rivet all her attention on the two-inch gap between the shade and the window sill.

The dark figure moved noiselessly across the room with no more substance than a shadow. It paused at the desk and flicked on a penlight. The tiny yellow pinpoint moved across the papers on the desk, then flicked off. The shadow moved and the dot of light scanned the mantle. Elizabeth held her breath as the shadow turned toward the balcony, then stopped at the low table by the sofa. The light zigged back and forth across the lines of her notebook, left open to the appropriate page. Then the light extinguished, and the shadow exited into the darkness. And for Elizabeth all the lights in the world were eclipsed.

15

Sunday

The next morning Elizabeth was thankful for the cover stick in her makeup bag, which hid the dark circles under her eyes. She considered forcing herself to drink a cup of strong black coffee, but decided her nervous system could provide all the energy she needed without artificial stimulation.

While all the teams were finding seats in the parlor, she cornered Irene and explained one addition she wanted to make to the script—a prologue—and asked Irene to set up the action with Richard and Benton.

Elizabeth's nervous tension mounted as she waited through the other team's presentations. The Circle did a rhythm play based on the children's game, "Who stole the cookies from the cookie jar?" Clapping and saying, "Who put the poison in Gloria's soup?" "Susie put the poison in Gloria's soup." "Who me?" "Yes, you." "Not

199

me." "Then who?" "Nigel put . . . " until they came down to the conclusion that "Millie put the poison in Gloria's soup," and a team member portraying Millie confessed.

Private Lives draped the stage in sheets to depict Mount Olympus and did a sketch with a Zeus, who threw lightning bolts and wreaked judgment on Brian Rielly for betraying the trust his country placed in him, for killing his partner in double-dealing espionage, and for allowing his—surprise!—*wife*, Susie, to take the rap.

Another team produced a television set and presented a videotaped drama; another did a parody of a Broadway musical; another a TV show, "This is Your Death, Gloria Glitz." Two of the plays were all in rhyme.

Elizabeth's tension mounted as the minutes dragged on, until she felt that she was trapped in some kind of timeless purgatory where her punishment was to watch an interminable amount of lighthearted cavorting on the stage, never knowing when her number would be called, never being free of the burden of what she must do.

"Our next solution will be presented by Blithe Spirit." Stark's announcement finally ended her agony.

Clutching her script with clammy hands, her heart thudding so she thought she couldn't breathe, let alone speak, Elizabeth walked to the microphone as Irene set a small table and two chairs on the stage. Richard and Benton sat down with a large bottle labeled *Brandy* between them.

Lord, you promised the disciples you'd get them to the other side, and you did. My boat is sinking fast—get me to the other side, please, she prayed. Immediately her mind was filled with a picture of the white-robed Christ, his arms upraised, telling her emotional storm, "Peace. Be still."

And it was.

"Truth Is Stranger than Fiction." Elizabeth announced the title of their skit, then cleared her throat before proceeding. "Two years ago at White's in London, American thriller writer Weldon Stark entertained his acquaintance Sir Gavin Kendall with eighty-proof brandy and cleverly plotted mystery stories." The actors pantomimed animated drinking and conversing.

"Not to be outdone, Sir Gavin countered with a story even more diabolically intricate. There were only two problems with the situation: Sir Gavin was too drunk to remember what he had told, but his friend wasn't; and the plot was not fiction, but an incredibly involved true-life drama in which Sir Gavin Kendall himself was the prime actor." Puzzle pieces danced onto the stage, highlighting Elizabeth's words with their movement.

"With the aid of her detective-inspector uncle, a night school composition instructor, and tidbits she had learned working for her mystery-writer boss, Victoria Parkerson wrote the first draft of a blockbuster mystery novel, but died of cancer before she could do anything more with it.

"Only one copy of the manuscript existed, and Victoria had given it to her half sister Mildred to read. Mildred, maid to actress Margo Lovell— better known to the present company as Gloria Glitz—left the bundle of papers around Margo's dressing room where the actress found it and devised an insidious scheme for attaining her most cherished goal: becoming the mistress of a titled fortune.

"Margo gave a photocopy of the story to her mystery writer friend, assuring him the author was dead and encouraging him to rewrite it and publish it under his own name. The success of *Who Doth Murder Sleep?* is literary history.

"The death of Margo's uncle, James Lovell, provided the perfect hiding place for the key ingredient in her plan: the manuscript. She secreted it inside the casket before it was sealed in the family vault. There it would lie forever hidden unless she, as the next of kin, should seek an order for exhumation, which she was confident the newly knighted Sir Gavin would not be so uncooperative as to require of her.

"A rational man, Sir Gavin readily saw that reason was the better part of valor and so bowed to Margo's demands, being too well bred to call them by the ugly name of blackmail. He broke his long-standing but unofficial engagement to

Lady Leila Landsbury and prepared to acquiesce to his blackmailer's monetary and matrimonial demands. But as her noose tightened around his life, he began to puzzle over possible routes of escape."

The puzzle pieces bumped together in unsuccessful attempts to achieve a perfect fit as the narration continued: "Still Margo held the key piece. And with no possibility of recovering it, his only chance of escape lay in removing Margo. Nigel Cass's storm-battered dinner party provided the perfect opportunity for Sir Gavin—our Linden Leigh—to introduce his own solution to the puzzle. A solution of 50 milligrams of cyanide, innocently supplied by his chemist brother-in-law.

"The fact that Margo's agent had peopled his guest list with those bearing grudges against the glamorous actress—whatever similarity they may or may not have borne to our present cast—added a certain poetically ironic touch to the occasion. But the ultimate irony was performed by Sir Gavin as he secretly emptied the contents of a cyanide capsule onto the rim of the glass he was to hold to his fiancée's lips with his own hand, after pretending to drink from it himself in honor of their engagement.

"The care given to every detail of the plot showed in several things: his anonymous request that almond soup be served, to cover the bitter almond smell of the cyanide; his quick response to administer aid to his victim's choking symptoms; and in the rapidly performed cremation following the village doctor's certificate of natural death.

"And that would have been the end of the matter—" The puzzle pieces started to come together, then paused—"had it not been for Victoria's uncle, Detective-Inspector Parkerson of Scotland Yard." The puzzle pieces reeled apart in confusion.

"As soon as Parkerson read *Who Doth Murder Sleep*—" The eyes pantomimed reading, looked at each other questioningly, then nodded—"he recognized his niece's work. To the mind of a trained detective, it wasn't hard to figure out what had happened to the manuscript that had disappeared from Victoria's personal effects. But without the original, he had no proof.

"Parkerson was more intrigued than surprised when he read of Margo Lovell's death. After all, the pieces fit so well—especially after he had a nice long chat with his stepniece, Mildred, and then read the death certificate mentioning cherry-red lividity, which he recognized as a symptom of cyanide poisoning.

"But again, he had no proof. He lacked the essential key we have given you—knowledge of where the original manuscript was hidden. For that original would have been his proof of motive. Parkerson's retirement from Scotland Yard occurred that year, but he didn't retire from the puzzle of proving Margo's murder and, more important to him, gaining posthumous recognition of his niece's genius.

"The puzzle became a passionate obsession to him as he dogged Sir Gavin, even openly accusing the writer of his twin crimes of plagiarism and murder. But Sir Gavin knew both his victims were safely buried in the family vault.

"Not until late this past Saturday did the maze of defenses begin to crumble when Sir Gavin Kendall arrived to rehearse 'Murder by Candlelight' and learned the plot Weldon Stark was using for his mystery. Shaken, but confident of carrying everything off as the fiction Stark believed it to be, Sir Gavin met his nemesis, when, upon exiting from the parlor, he glimpsed Charles Parkerson leaving the balcony of the rehearsal room, flushed with the information he had sought so doggedly for four years.

"In a show of losing with good sportsmanship in the best stiff-upper-lip style, Kendall invited Parkerson to his room for a drink, or possibly a confession. Then, easily overpowering the older man, Gavin smothered him with a pillow, removed all identification, and dumped the body in a bathroom in an unused wing of the hotel—"

The dancing shapes did their final pirouette.

"—Where the body was discovered by the sleuths you see before you. They studied the clues, thought out the riddle, and found that the pieces fit." The forms came together making a giant likeness of Gavin Kendall. "The Puzzle is solved."

The room filled with confused applause from spectators, who weren't sure whether the elaborate solution was an attempt to win the originality prize or the answer to an actual murder. But Elizabeth was only dimly aware of the perplexed disorder around her. For the first time she allowed her gaze to seek out Gavin.

He was a figure of quiet in a roomful of uproar. Gavin didn't move. Neither did the policeman standing at the back of the parlor. And the full horror of what she had done hit Elizabeth. She had publicly accused an innocent man of horrible crimes. She had embarrassed him unforgivably, and she had forever sealed her fate, cutting herself off irrevocably from the love he had offered her.

If only she could call back her words, turn back time, rearrange the puzzle pieces. The least she could do—a useless, futile gesture, but the only possible thing—was to go to him and apologize.

As she made her way slowly through the room abuzz with discussions of what she had just said, people saw her coming and moved aside, clearing a path to Gavin like the waters of the Red Sea.

She crossed to him on dry sand.

"Gavin, I'm so sorry . . . " She could think of nothing else to say.

"O thou invisible spirit of wine, if thou hast no name to be known by let us call thee devil! . . . O God, that men should put an enemy in their mouths to steal away their brains! . . . Every inordinate cup is unblessed, the ingredient is a devil."

She gasped at his quotation, not sure she heard him right. "Gavin?"

"It was the wine that spoke and not the man, but *en vino veritas.*"

"It is true." She wasn't sure if she spoke the words aloud, but they were accompanied by a noise as loud to her ears as the crack of a gun— the bursting of her bubble of dreams. She didn't realize until that moment, until she heard the confession from his own lips, that she had still clung to the tiniest hope that she'd been wrong.

"Not very sporting of me, was it?" He dug in his vest pocket for his eyepiece. "Broke the old public school code and all that, what? Pity you couldn't see your way clear to accept my offer, old girl. I really meant it, you know. Wouldn't want you to think I was a cad about that, too. I could have made a better show of it with your help."

Elizabeth glanced uncomfortably around her and saw, thankfully, that Stark was calling everyone's attention to the front of the room—giving them a semblance of privacy. She turned back to Gavin, all of her might-have-been feelings swelling to the bursting point. "No you wouldn't, Gavin. No person can make that change in another. People can't change themselves by deciding to turn over a new leaf—"

She choked on her last words. She didn't want to preach to him, she wanted to rail at the evil that had insidiously induced him to choose the first step of plagiarism, then murder in an attempt to extricate himself from its clutches, and then a second murder in a desperate attempt to escape the tightening web.

Suddenly she knew what to say. "Another person can't do it for you, Gavin, but you can change—with God's help. It's up to you."

The monocle slipped from his fingers as he looked at her intently for just a moment. Then he picked it up again and turned to a figure just behind Elizabeth. "Well, cheerio."

Elizabeth turned to look beside her. "Anita?"

"Special agent, Chaffee County Sheriff's Office." Anita held out an ID card. "Parkerson checked in with our office early Saturday morning, and I was assigned to meet him here that night. Unfortunately, I was too late." She signaled to the officer in the doorway who moved forward to read the suspect his rights. "Thank you for all your help, Richard." They shook hands in a businesslike manner.

Then Elizabeth felt the strength in Richard's

hands as he took her arm and guided her from the room. All the way to their rooms, she drew on the resource of that strength.

Inside their parlor, Richard touched a match to the newly laid fire and pulled Elizabeth to its warmth. Suddenly she was talking, not sure what she was saying, not caring whether or not it made sense, just telling Richard everything she had seen and heard and thought and worried about in the past days. He held her and listened without interruption until all her words were spent and she leaned against him for support.

"I wonder why he didn't run when he read the script?" Richard said. "He could be in Mexico by now."

"Oh, I didn't leave the real one out. The script on the table was the alternate I'd worked out in case he didn't prove me right by taking my bait. I kept hoping one of the other suspects would come." She swallowed down the lump in her throat. "But Gavin came. Oh, Richard—"

Richard held her, gently stroking her hair. When she seemed calmer he said, "How did you know his excuse for moving the body was false?"

"His whole story was built around the fact that no one could do anything until the police came anyway. But when they did get here, he didn't tell them. I was there when they took his statement."

Richard nodded. "Would cyanide really work the way it did in the skit?"

"I don't know. I suppose Stark simplified it for dramatic effect, same as he changed the time period for fun. But the essentials were right." She choked as a new wave of the horror of it all hit her.

"If only I hadn't been right. I prayed to be wrong. Richard—"

He held her tightly, pushing the horror back with his own fierce caring. At last he said with his lips against her ear, "'Let love be genuine; hate what is evil, hold fast to what is good.'"

She nodded, the top of her head brushing his cheek. "Yes, Paul was right on the mark when he wrote that to the Romans, wasn't he? It's just like I read this morning, 'The villain's ways are villainous and he devises infamous plans to ruin the poor with his lies and deny justice to the needy. But the man of noble mind forms noble designs and stands firm in his nobility.'"

In the comfort of Richard's arms it all became clear to her who the man of noble mind was. Elizabeth realized that it was Richard's presence that held her steady during the landslide. She knew now that the night on the balcony while Richard and Gavin chased the fictional jewel thief, it was Richard whose safety she was praying for. And that one, brief moment when she thought Richard might be involved had been much more shattering to her world than learning the whole truth about Gavin. It was Richard. It had always been Richard.

Now she saw it. Richard was of the true nobility, the real gentleman who put the rights and feelings of others before his own.

Now she knew. She knew the difference between love and infatuation. Between dreams and reality. She realized her feelings for Gavin had been based on fantasy and superficial qualities, and that she had made a vital error in deciding to trust Gavin because she loved him—basing her decision on advice from a novel rather than from the Bible.

She looked up at the outline of Richard's profile—how unspeakably dear to her he was!—and realized that what she had considered his dullness was one of his most endearing qualities. Richard was real, dependable, solid . . .

Besides, he's not nearly as dull as I used to think. For the first time that day, she smiled.

She knew what she would answer the next time he asked her to marry him.

But would he ask?

How long had it been since the last time? It seemed like a lifetime—just before she met Gavin . . . and Richard met Anita.

Would he ask again? She had had so many chances and blown them all. Nobody got that many second chances. Now that she knew Richard was the real hero for her, would he want the part?

His voice broke her reverie. "Are you feeling better now?"

"Yes, my lord."

He held her at arms' length and looked at her. "What did you say?"

"You heard me," she laughed.

"I say, are you casting me as your fictional hero now?" He adjusted an imaginary monocle.

"Oh, no!" She leaned up on her tiptoes and kissed his cheek. "I've got a much better role in mind for you."

"Do you really mean it?"

"More than I've ever meant anything." She moved back so she could watch his face as she spoke. "It was you all along, Richard, only I didn't realize it."

He held his arms open to her. "Let's go home."

Home—it spoke of comfort, of protection, of freedom . . . of Richard. She walked into his arms. "I'm already there."

Epilogue

Elizabeth walked into Richard's office carrying a bowl of April daffodils and tulips. He looked up from the letter he was reading. "It's from Bill. He wants to make sure we put next year's mystery week on our calendars now. It looks as if the whole group plans to return. This year will be a hard act to follow, though. We can't hope to win that big every time."

Elizabeth put the flowers on his desk and walked around to plant herself on his lap. "Shall we invite them all to our wedding? Irene and Cathy would make darling bridesmaids . . . I don't know about Anita—"

"You aren't still worried about her, are you? You said you believed me when I explained it was all to provide a cover for her investigations."

"Even the kiss in the gazebo? That was all in the line of duty?"

"The fact that you believed it was real proves it was effective camouflage, doesn't it? Anita had her suspicions about Gavin pretty well worked out by then, and we were worried about your safety."

"Poor Gavin." She stood up and moved around the room. "It's still so hard to believe . . . "

Richard nodded, but characteristically didn't interrupt her stream of thought.

"Was I wrong to dream?"

"Of course not. Dreaming the impossible dream is part of the human spirit. After all, if you don't have a dream, you can't have a dream come true."

She laughed. "You sound like a show tune writer."

"Yes, I guess I do. Sorry. But the point is to dream your dreams—then redeem them in the light of reality." He stood and walked to her. "Elizabeth, in the hard, cold light of day are you disappointed in your bargain?"

She flung her arms around his neck. "Richard! Don't you ever think such a thing! All my heart is yours, and all my dreams are of you."

When he kissed her she knew the fulfillment of the promise that the redeemed would come home, entering the Promised Land with shouts of triumph, crowned with everlasting gladness. "And gladness and joy will be their escort."

She rested her head against his chest. "I was right all along: dreams can come true. But the pearl of great price may be in your own backyard."

"Well . . ." Richard leaned down and nibbled at her ear. "If you find things getting dull, we can always go to another mystery week."

"Mmmm, maybe." She lifted her face and traced the line of his cheek with her finger. "But I have a feeling the real world will be quite exciting enough."

THE END